e.

Class II.	From.	To.	Class III.	From.	To.	Class IV.
Grammar Lesson	IX. 50	X. 30	Grammar Lesson	IX. 50	XI. 10	Lesson with Revd. H. Baber.
Reading.	X. 30	XI. 40	Reading.	XI. 10	XI. 40	Grammar Lesson
Arithmetic. Mr. Tate.	XI. 40	I.	Arithmetic. Mr. Tate.	XI. 40	I.	Arithmetic. Mr. Tate.
Needle-work.			Needle-work.	II	IV. 10	Needle-work.
Singing. Mr. May.	II.	IV. 10				
Needle-work.	IV. 10.	V.	Copy Books.	IV. 10.	V.	Copy Books.
Geography Lesson.	IX. 50	XI. 10	Lesson with Revd. H. Baber	IX. 50	X. 30	Geography Lesson.
Paraphrase.	XI. 10.	XII.	Geography Lesson	X. 30	XI. 20	Reading
Reading.	I. 30	II. 30	Singing. Mr. May.	XI. 20	XII.	Dictation.
Needle-work.	II. 30	III. 30	Needle-work	I. 30	II. 30	Singing. Mr. May.
History Lesson.	III. 30	III. 50	Dictation	II. 30	IV.	Needle-work.
Copy Books.	III. 50	IV. 30	Write an Exercise	IV.	IV. 30	Copy Books.
Lesson with Rev. H. Baber.	IX. 50	X. 40	Grammar Lesson	IX. 50	X. 40.	Reading
Grammar Lesson.	X. 40	XI. 10.	Reading.	X. 40	XI. 10	Grammar Lesson.
	XI. 10.	XII.	Prepare a Lesson	XI. 10	XII.	Prepare a Lesson.
Lesson with Mr. Hullah.	II.	IV.	Needle-work.	II.	IV.	Needle-work.
Needle-work.	IV.	IV. 30.	Reading	IV.	IV. 30	Write in Copy Books.
	IV. 30	V.	Repeat a Lesson.	IV. 30	V.	Repeat a Lesson.
Geography Lesson.	IX. 50	X. 30	Geography Lesson.	IX. 50	X. 50	Lesson with Revd. H. Baber.
Poetry.	X. 30	X. 50	Write from Memory	X. 50	I.	Arithmetic. Mr. Tate.
Arithmetic. Mr. Tate.	X. 50	I.	Arithmetic. Mr. Tate.			Needle-work.
Needle-work.	II.	III. 30	Needle-work	II.	III. 30	
Singing. Mr. May.	III.	IV. 30	Model Lesson.	III. 30	IV. 30	Model Lesson
Model Lesson.			Copy Books.	IV. 30	V.	Copy Books.
Write an Exercise.	IV. 30	V.				
Grammar Lesson	IX. 50	XI. 10	Lesson with Rev. H. Baber	IX. 50	X. 30	Grammar Lesson.
History.	XI. 30	XII.	History Lesson.	X. 30	XI.	Prophecies.
Reading.	I. 30	II. 30	Singing. Mr. May.	XI	XI. 30	History Lesson.
Needle-work.	II. 30	III. 30	Needle-work	XI. 30	XII.	Dictation.
Revd. H. Baber's Exercise.	III. 30	IV. 30	Revd. H. Baber's Exercise	I. 30	II. 30	Singing. Mr. May.
Copy Books.				II. 30	III. 30	Needle-work.
				III. 30	IV. 30	Revd. H. Baber's Exercise.

For Revd. H. Baber August 11th 1848.

THE STORY OF
ROEHAMPTON UNIVERSITY

THE STORY OF
ROEHAMPTON
UNIVERSITY

NIGEL WATSON

THIRD MILLENNIUM
PUBLISHING, LONDON

© 2010 Roehampton University and
Third Millennium Publishing Limited

First published in 2010 by Third Millennium Publishing Limited,
a subsidiary of Third Millennium Information Limited.

2–5 Benjamin Street
London
United Kingdom
EC1M 5QL
www.tmiltd.com

THIRD MILLENNIUM
PUBLISHING. LONDON

ISBN 978 1 906507 13 8

British Library Cataloguing in Publication Data:
A CIP catalogue record for this book is available from the British Library.

Written by Nigel Watson
Edited by Susan Millership
Picture Research by Susan Millership
Designed by Matthew Wilson
Production by Bonnie Murray
Reprographics by Studio Fasoli, Italy
Printed by Scotprint, Scotland

CONTENTS

FOREWORD

I am grateful to have been asked to write a few words of introduction to this first-ever history of Roehampton University as it gives me a chance to share with a wider audience my enthusiasm for the University.

When I became Chancellor in 2005 I knew a little about the University, as it is based quite close to where I live, and remembered that it had a very strong background in teacher training and education. But it was only when I first came to visit and to meet the staff and students that I began to gain a real sense of the place, its culture and its richness. For example I was immediately impressed by how friendly and welcoming everyone was and how broad the curriculum now is, with strengths in areas such as dance, anthropology, drama and history. It has also moved into newer areas of study and research with topics such as film, creative writing and journalism, which are of course dear to my own heart.

But I also learned how ambitious the University was for its future, with new projects in India, Malaysia, the United States and Europe and, through its work with

Left: John Simpson talking to a student.

Opposite: Students at graduation outside Guildford Cathedral.

the private sector, demonstrating a commitment to preparing its students to be global citizens as well as finding new ways of funding its activities – an imperative in the straitened financial times that we now live in.

Reading this history has given me a new perspective on all these things – how the buildings that are part of this beautiful campus carry their own fascinating stories, some of them a little scandalous, others simply very human stories of bravery or stoicism during the wars. The commitment to culture and to social justice that is such an important and vibrant part of the University as it is today, is also part of the historic legacy from the colleges and their providing bodies. All of these things add to the richness of *The Story of Roehampton University*.

In what is now over 40 years of reporting for the BBC, I have witnessed some extraordinary events: the end of apartheid in South Africa and the wars in Kosovo, Afghanistan and Iraq. In my work I have seen first hand the immense danger that comes when people don't communicate properly with each other, don't understand each other, and can't or won't respect people with different ways of seeing the world.

Which is why I believe so strongly that bringing people together from around the world, so that they learn together in a spirit of internationalism, is one of the most important ways of ensuring that we seize the positive opportunities that are presented by globalization. And that is exactly the vision that drives Roehampton and why universities like ours have such an important role to play in this rapidly changing and unpredictable world.

I never tire of saying just how delighted I am to be part of Roehampton University and I always take every opportunity to talk to people I meet in my work about the great work that this University does.

This history gives me another opportunity to say that and to say it loudly.

John Simpson, Chancellor, Roehampton University

Author Acknowledgements

The history of Roehampton University is the history of the development of modern British universities. The history of the constituent colleges has been well recorded and I am hugely indebted to the authors of those histories, particularly Peter Weston, Eileen Foster, John Seed and Malcolm Cole. The story of the creation of Roehampton Institute of Higher Education and its development into an independent university has not been so well covered. I have been reliant in particular on the college archivists, whose collections have contained not only college papers but also papers for the Institute and University not held elsewhere, and I would like to thank in particular Eileen Foster, Gilly King and Stuart Brenner. Gilly King also kindly organized a questionnaire for former students of Whitelands which provided valuable insights into the changing perceptions of students over the years. I would also like to thank Kornelia Keepok for access to the Froebel College archive held in the University Library. Peter Weston was also most helpful in providing a broad overview of the development of Roehampton since the 1970s. So too were the many people who kindly agreed to be interviewed and I would like to thank Raywen Ford, Paul Hodges, David Woodman, Andy Skinner, Paul O'Prey, Peter Weston, Geoffrey Walker, John Seed, Neil Taylor, Pauline Perry, Jen Coates, Peter Briggs, Zachary Leader, Dorothy Bell, Jane Read, Sue Robson, Bernie Porter, Andy Masheter, David Peacock, Robin Headlam-Wells, Trevor Dean and Lucy Whelan. The brief bibliography at the end of the book lists the items I found most helpful in my research.

Nigel Watson
Summer 2010

Students walking through the Wisteria Walk, Grove House.

INTRODUCTION

Established in 2004, Roehampton University is one of the UK's newest universities yet one with old roots. The origins of the University's four colleges – Whitelands, Southlands, Digby Stuart and Froebel – lie in the nineteenth century, the oldest, Whitelands, being founded in 1841. The international reputation of the University's outstanding school of education owes much to the colleges' pioneering work over more than a century in the training of teachers. Yet, while teacher training remains an important part of the University's work, education at Roehampton today offers so much more, with a wide range of courses covering areas such as early childhood studies, special and inclusive education, and education leadership and management.

This is typical of the diversity and richness of the programmes studied by the University's nearly 9,000 students. They are taught by some outstanding academics, leaders in their field, with strengths in many subjects, notably in areas such as English literature, linguistics, dance, history, biological sciences and anthropology. In a remarkably short time the calibre of the University's research as well as its teaching has earned for Roehampton a reputation as one of the UK's leading modern universities.

It is a reputation that attracts as diverse a range of students as the courses offered by the University. There is no such thing as a

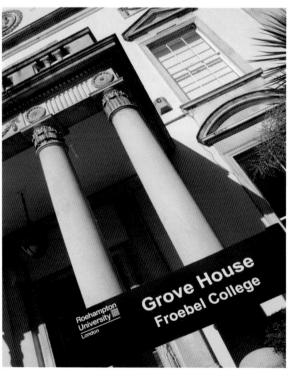

Top right: Fountain in the grounds of Grove House.

Far right: Grove House, the home of Froebel College.

Right: Digby Stuart.

10

Top: Architectural shot of Parkstead House, Whitelands.

Above: The Queen's Building, Southlands.

typical Roehampton student. They come from a wide variety of different backgrounds, from nearby London neighbourhoods, from the Home Counties, as well as from all over the UK and many other countries. The University hosts students of more than 130 different nationalities, of all races and religions. Among the undergraduate and post-graduate population are full-time students who have just left school as well as mature students studying part-time. One of Roehampton's attractions is the vibrancy created by such a rich mix.

Small, friendly and collegiate, Roehampton has the additional advantage of being London's only campus university. The extensive landscaped and tree-filled grounds which make up the Roehampton Lane site and the Whitelands site, a short walk away at Parkstead House, form a green oasis amid the urban landscape of greater London yet give easy access to the centre of the capital with all its attractions. This advantage is enhanced by the community atmosphere stemming from the four constituent colleges which make Roehampton the only modern collegiate university.

This then is the story of the continuing evolution of a modern university but one which still takes pride in an ethos of education that owes much to those College pioneers of more than a century ago.

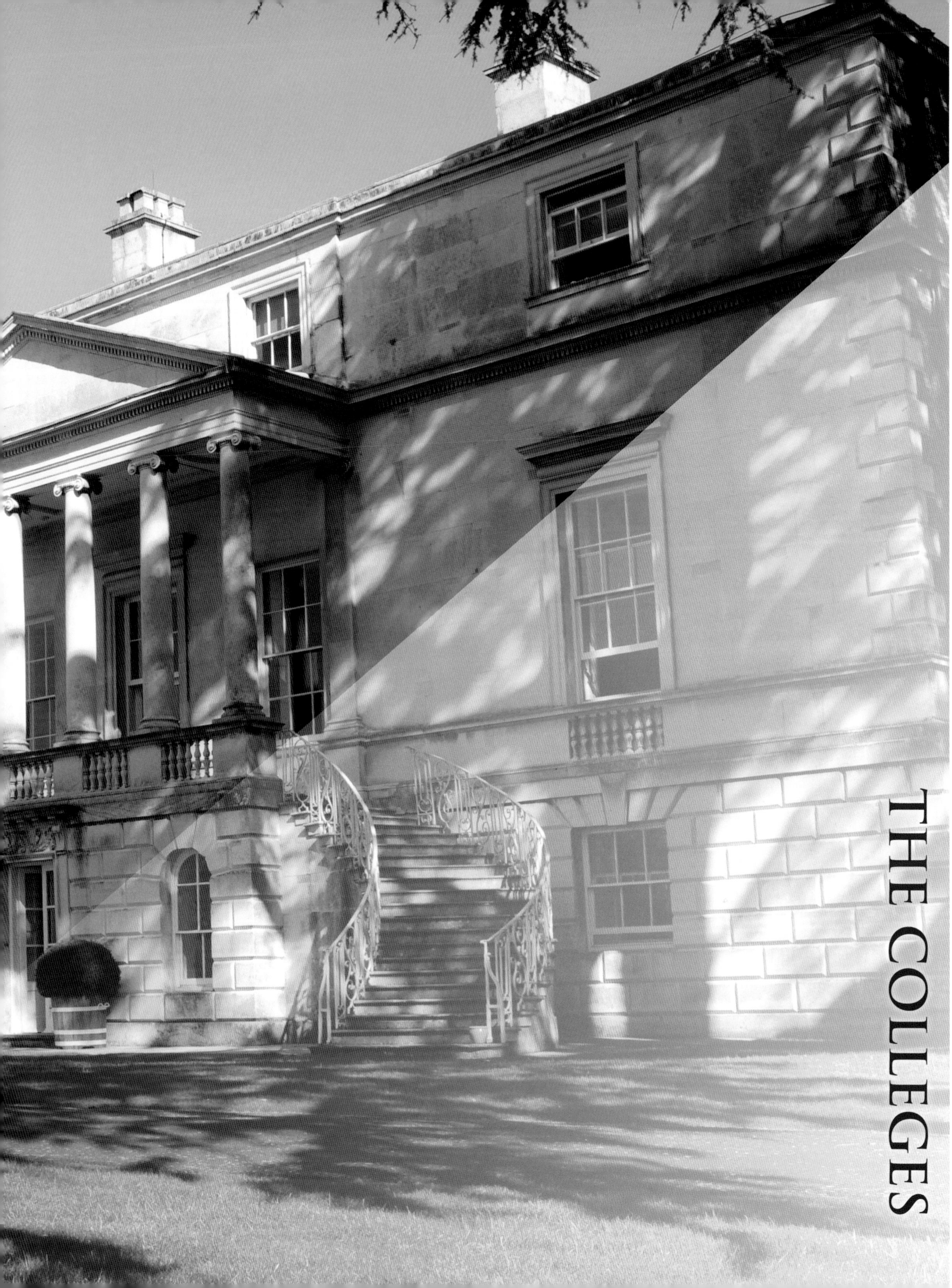

PART 1

THE COLLEGES

EARLY HISTORY
1800–1900

Three of Roehampton's four colleges, Whitelands, Southlands and Digby Stuart, were established because the churches which founded them wanted to retain an influential role in mass education as the British state became increasingly involved. The fourth, Froebel, was completely non-denominational, formed to promote the pioneering child-centred educational philosophy of the Prussian Friedrich Froebel, from whom it took its name. Yet all four voluntary colleges still had much in common. In training elementary school teachers they gave educational and professional advantages to a class of women who would otherwise have been denied such opportunities. They also shared a determination to raise the calibre of elementary school teachers, and as a consequence the standard of education in elementary schools. And, despite their differing backgrounds and distinctive characters, they shared a similar ethos, based on strict discipline and a rigid curriculum, which nevertheless encouraged a strong mutual bond between many students, creating a source of strength in a career which often left them socially isolated.

Whitelands College, Chelsea.

Above: A postcard showing Whitelands College's first location on King's Road, Chelsea.

Opposite: Detail from the stained glass window of St Ursula designed by Edward Burne-Jones for Whitelands chapel in 1882.

Previous spread: Whitelands College was founded in 1841. It moved to its present site at Parkstead House in 2004.

Founded in 1841, Whitelands was the first of Roehampton's four colleges. The first all-women teacher-training college, it took its name from its first home, Whitelands House, in King's Road, Chelsea. It was established by the National Society for the Promotion of the Education of the Poor in the Principles of the Established Church. An Anglican organization formed in 1811, the National Society had been one of the two main bodies providing elementary schools for the poor, the other being the non-conformist British & Foreign Schools Society, formed in 1808.

The National Society first began training teachers in 1813 but the quality of this training came under increasing criticism. In response, the Society founded two central training colleges in London, one for men, St Mark's, and the other for women, Whitelands. The first 12 Whitelands students arrived in January 1842, their numbers increasing within a few years to more than 50. This might seem small but in 1845 there were just 540 students in all 22 Church training colleges, with the largest, Battersea, having 71.

By 1870 the limited impact of voluntary religious organizations on elementary education was evident. Sixty per cent of all children aged between six and ten and 80 per cent of all those between ten and twelve were not on school registers. A third of all women and a fifth of all men were still illiterate. The 1870 Education Act was passed to remedy this situation, providing state elementary schools in areas where voluntary provision was inadequate. By the 1890s municipal school boards managed 5,000 elementary schools. At the same time the Act stimulated an increase of 50 per cent in the number of voluntary schools. Between 1872 and 1901 these rose from 9,800 to 14,000, with the Church of England doubling the number under its control from 6,000 to 12,000. This increase placed a huge strain on the existing teacher-training system, especially since school boards were banned from running their own training colleges. As a result, many schools relied on a rising number of untrained teachers, either pupil-teachers or assistant teachers, that is, former pupil-teachers who had not attended training colleges. By the 1890s at least half of all women and a quarter of all men teaching in board schools had no college training. This had clear implications for the quality of education given in elementary schools and demonstrated an urgent need for the voluntary societies to expand their own training colleges.

Early Southlands students at the College's first premises in Battersea.

Right: Statue of St Madeleine Sophie Barat in the Digby Stuart Chapel holding a model of the Elm Grove estate.

Below: Elm Grove house in 1804.

Whitelands responded by taking in more students. By 1878, with 140 students, it was the largest training college in the country. At the same time new voluntary teacher-training colleges were founded. Westminster College, the only one run by the Wesleyan Education Committee (WEC), was unable to cope with the demand for new teachers. As a result, a new college for female students only, the Southlands Wesleyan Training College, was opened in Battersea in 1872. The WEC had been formed in 1838 to manage the hundred or so Wesleyan day schools. Westminster College had been opened in 1851 as a mixed but segregated college. Southlands was based closely on Westminster, with a training year running from February until December, punctuated by several short vacations. It was only in 1895 that training colleges generally altered their academic year to run in parallel with that of the universities, starting in autumn and ending in summer.

The Catholic Church too was expanding its capacity for training teachers. At the time there were only two Catholic teacher-training colleges in England and Wales – Mount Pleasant in Liverpool, founded for women in 1852, and Hammersmith in London, founded for men in 1850. Archbishop Manning tried to persuade the Religious of the Holy Child Jesus to set up a new college in Westminster but they lacked the resources to do so. Another order, the Society of the Sacred Heart, which had been running a school for Catholic girls in Roehampton since 1850, was eager to take up the challenge, but Manning was reluctant. More concerned with educating children from the families of recently arrived Irish immigrants, he was suspicious of the Society's links with upper-class Catholicism. Led by the determined Mother Mabel Digby, the Society was not easily deterred, turning instead to the neighbouring Catholic diocese of Southwark, whose bishop proved much more sympathetic. The chance to set up a training college was offered to the Society in 1873 and accepted in January 1874.

The Society of the Sacred Heart had acquired Elm Grove in Roehampton in 1850. Here, on a small estate of some 36 acres, the Society had established a convent with a private girls' boarding school. This would eventually become the home of what was ultimately called Digby Stuart College, and later still would

Above: Trainee school mistresses at West Hill in 1901.

Above right: West Hill, Wandsworth.

form the heart of the campus of the future university. Since hurried arrangements had to be made to receive the first 21 young women students, it was here too that the new training college began its life in February 1874. At the same time enquiries were being made for separate premises and in July 1874 the college moved to The Orchards, West Hill, Wandsworth, under Mother Charlotte Leslie as the first Principal. Officially called the Training College of the Sacred Heart for Catholic Schoolmistresses, it became known as Wandsworth College. By the early 1890s there were 99 students in residence, drawn from all over the country, with a small number of Irish and Maltese students.

Beyond the boundary wall of Elm Grove and the cloistered grounds of the Society of the Sacred Heart's convent lay another small estate, Grove House. Eventually, in 1922, this would become the home of the fourth of the Roehampton colleges, Froebel College. But like the other three, Froebel, when it opened in January 1895, was based some miles away from Roehampton. On the other hand, it was the only one whose premises, in Talgarth Road and Colet Gardens, West Kensington, were purpose-built. Initially Froebel was also non-residential. The biggest contrast lay in Froebel's non-denominational character.

The College was founded and run by the Froebel Educational Institute. Formed in 1892, the Institute was part of an expanding Froebel network in the United Kingdom. This included the Froebel Society, established in 1874, and the National Froebel Union, set up in 1887. All this was done to promote the child-centred, play-based educational philosophy of Friedrich Froebel, the Prussian educationist and founder of the kindergarten, who died in 1852. After the Prussian state closed down all the Froebel kindergartens in 1851, fearful of their association with Froebel's liberal, republican and anti-authoritarian views, his supporters sought refuge in Britain. The first kindergarten in the UK was opened in London in 1851. The enthusiastic promotion of Froebel's

Left: Kindergarten pupils being taught by Miss Esther Lawrence, Froebel Principal, 1901–31.

Below: Examples of Froebel's teaching equipment or 'gifts'.

ideas and the standing of many of his key supporters influenced several day training centres and training colleges, including Southlands and Wandsworth, to adopt part of his philosophy. The Institute was formed to extend Froebel's ideas beyond infant education and train the teachers who would carry this out. The new College offered two courses, leading to the award of the elementary and higher certificates validated by the National Froebel Union. But rather than the elementary schools – the focus of the training in the other three colleges – the training at Froebel was, in the words of Peter Weston, the College's historian and the former Deputy Vice-Chancellor of the University, 'really directed at managing small groups of children in independent schools, rather than the very large classes of 50–70 in the board schools'.

FRIEDRICH FROEBEL

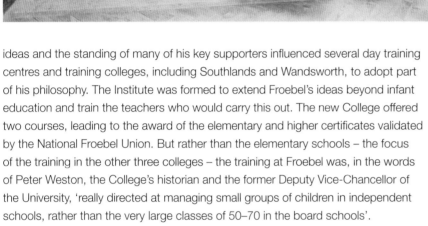

Froebel, the founder of the kindergarten movement, was born in Thuringia in Germany in 1782. A devout Christian, with a deep love of nature, be began teaching in 1805. He was heavily influenced by the ideas of Pestalozzi, under whom he studied in Switzerland. In 1816 he founded his own educational institute and in 1826 published his principal work on education, The Education of Man. In the 1830s he began concentrating on his greatest work, the education of pre-school children. His radical belief that the first learning experiences of the very young were crucial for their future education and for the well-being of society became hugely influential. Play was of central importance to this philosophy and Froebel himself made a range of play materials for young children. He founded a Play and Activity Institute in 1837, for which he coined the word 'kindergarten' in 1840. His views were too radical for the Prussian state which banned kindergartens in 1851, the year before Froebel's death. His philosophy, however, has flourished and, in an evolving form, continues to underpin the teaching of education for the very young in many parts of the world.

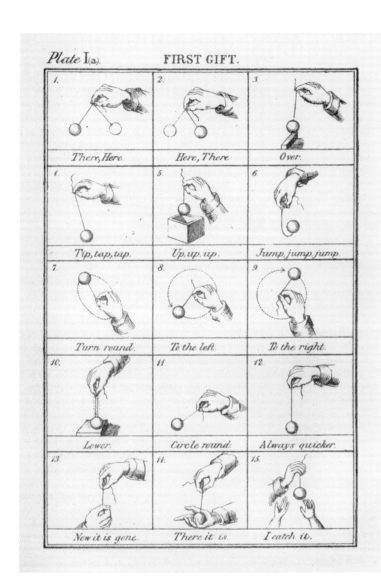

The four colleges nevertheless had more in common than they had differences. Over a period of more than half a century, they had been founded to train young women to teach young children. Whatever the character of their founding bodies, each college catered for a similar class of student, educated them according to a similar curriculum, inculcated a similar ethos and created a similar social bond between them.

At a time when middle-class women had few opportunities to take up a profession, teaching offered not only independence but also an escape from the social solitude and family constraints endured by many home-tied spinsters. Whitelands, in offering a route for such women into elementary teaching, predated other efforts being made to raise the standard of women's education around this time, such as the Governesses' Benevolent Institution, formed in 1843, which led to the creation of Queen's College in 1848. Whitelands set out to recruit well-to-do young women, deliberately setting

Above: Diagram from Froebel instruction book.

Top right: Educational games in the courtyard at Talgarth Road.

high fees to attract entrants of a similar social standing, but in fact most students in the early years of the College came from the lower middle class or the artisan working class, whose fathers were yeomen, shopkeepers or clerks. In the early 1850s one in five were orphans or the daughters of widows, despatched in the hope of securing better prospects in life. Many were drawn from the ranks of pupil-teachers, a system which began in 1846. Girls – and boys – were selected for such training at the age of 13, helping out with day-to-day classroom teaching and school management in exchange for instruction from the head of the school, for which they were paid a small wage. After five years they either took up a post as a teacher or strove for the

distinction of becoming a Queen's Scholar by examination, entitling them to attend a training college for two years. While Whitelands encouraged young women from the better-off middle classes to gain college places through the scholarship system, this revealed only that they were even more ignorant than their socially inferior peers who had come through the elementary school system, so dire was the way in which the daughters of the more affluent middle classes were educated.

By the 1870s when Southlands and Wandsworth were established, the colleges were receiving an initial entrance fee, fees for the two-year course and, finally, a grant from the state payable only after college graduates had completed two years in teaching. Many parents could afford to send their daughters to training college only by making financial sacrifices, for there was little financial support available, unless they had wealthy sponsors. Southlands and Wandsworth both drew their students from much the same pool as Whitelands. At Southlands, the first two students, Ellen Hollings and Annie Prowse, were both Queen's Scholars, as were those at Wandsworth, although they came to Wandsworth having failed to win places at the more prestigious Mount Pleasant. More than a third of students at Wandsworth also came from London with the remainder drawn fairly equally from the rest of the country, with some 20 per cent from the north, mainly those from the new influx of Catholic working-class families unable to win places at Mount Pleasant. Initially many Southlands students came from London but this changed with the opening of day training colleges in the capital, and instead Southlands took a growing number of students from the north, where Methodism was strong.

All three colleges were faced with the challenge of remedying the failure of the existing elementary school system to provide intending teachers with an adequate basic education. Whitelands, widely regarded as attracting the most able students, lamented in the College's annual report for 1870 that new students arrived 'unable to read with any clearness or efficiency and without the power of putting into simple language the little knowledge they possess'. Froebel faced the same situation more than a generation later.

Top left: Detail from stained glass window at Battersea which now hangs at Southlands College in Roehampton.

Top right: Pupils in a Froebel training school.

Above: Southlands students in Battersea playing croquet in the 1870s.

Right: Page from a 'College Friends' book, used to practice handwriting.

Below: Tug of war at Talgarth Road.

The poor elementary education received by students was blamed by the College for the pass rate recorded between 1900 and 1902 of just 70 per cent. The teaching to bring students up to scratch had to be squeezed in alongside instruction in school management, child development and learning methods as well as teaching practice, making the curriculum complex and overcrowded.

Most colleges offered teaching practice and experience through their own practising and demonstration schools. At Whitelands the dining room was turned into a practising school in 1844. At Southlands the practising school grew from 250 children to nearly 600 by the early 1880s. For most students, armed with their previous experience as pupil-teachers, teaching in front of enormous classes of 60 or more children held little fear. The weakness of this system was that it tended to confine teaching practice to the type of school set up by the college. This started to change towards the end of the century as colleges began using external schools. Students at Southlands were first taken to observe lessons at

other schools nearby in 1882 and from 1899 onwards were given a week's teaching practice in London Board schools. At Wandsworth, students were sent to the Sacred Heart elementary school in Roehampton and later to the Board school in Battersea and a high school in Wimbledon.

An overcrowded two-year training course led some of the colleges to consider adding a third year. This was first introduced at Whitelands, confined to a select handful of students, since it involved additional fees which few could afford. The College also encouraged the most able students to study for matriculation in the University of London, an examination equivalent to today's A levels established to determine the eligibility of students for university entrance. These students too, known as the 'University Students', were small in number, no more than 25 in the early 1900s. Southlands adopted the same practice, taking it one step further in 1900, when the best students were given the opportunity to take external degrees alongside their teaching certificate, staying at college for a third year to complete it. This practice continued until 1930.

As far as pedagogy itself was concerned, by the end of the century changing social attitudes were encouraging more progressive, child-centred approaches to teaching. The epitome of this was the course offered at Froebel. Although Froebel was not formally recognized as a training

Above: A miniature shirt sewn by a pupil of a trainee teacher.

Left: Teaching certificate issued for two years of 'normal training', 1871.

Below left: Trainee teacher with class in a Southlands practising school.

college until 1920, the Froebel teaching certificate was already widely accepted by 1900. Students at Southlands were among those at other colleges who were already studying for the Froebel certificate in kindergarten teaching. At Wandsworth model lessons based on kindergarten teaching were organized during the 1890s. Courses became less narrowly focused. The one which emerged at Southlands was typical, with more time for teaching practice and the inclusion of the history of education and the psychological and ethical aspects of education.

By the end of the century women had taken over many of the senior management posts in the colleges from men and dominated the teaching staffs. Most women at a senior level were professionally qualified and they encouraged their staff to improve their own qualifications. When Whitelands was founded, for instance, although there was a lady superintendent, and governesses supervised daily routine, most of the lecturers were local churchmen and the key figure was the chaplain, who became regarded as the de facto Principal. Similarly, at Southlands, while women administered the domestic routine of the College, senior management posts were held by men. Froebel, as so often, was different, partly because it

PASSIFLORA SERRATIFOLIA.
Passifloraceae
(near Cucurbit)

was founded rather later, when opinions were shifting. The moving force behind the College was Julia Salis Schwabe while the first Principal was another strong-minded woman, Emilie Michaelis.

All the College Principals promoted the constant improvement of teaching standards. Those women who first taught at the colleges lacked the advantages they were offering to their students. It was understandable that many of the colleges should wish to appoint to their staff recently qualified students but this did foster a culture which rarely looked beyond college boundaries for inspiration. It was only with the growing success of the campaign to improve educational opportunities for women, of which the training colleges were a part, that standards began to improve. In the 1870s, for instance, colleges for women were opened at both Oxford and Cambridge and women were at last admitted as students in the University of London. With competition from the new day training colleges linked with the universities and encouragement from the schools inspectorate, the colleges began to improve the professional standards of their staff. In 1886 staff at Whitelands were listed for the first time as affiliated to

Right: *May Day Procession of Queen Eva* at Whitelands College, painted by Anna Richards, 1902.

Below: Whitelands timetable showing students rising at 6am to wash, dress and sweep rooms followed by Scripture and prayers before breakfast at 8.30am. Bedtime was at 9pm.

the University of London and by the early 1890s all the College's governesses had matriculated as external students of the University. Over the next decade graduates would appear on the staff of all the colleges.

Student life was tightly controlled and strictly disciplined. The colleges were acting as the guardians of the young women in their care who would not reach their majority until they were 21. Most students would never have been away from home before and, in an era when society had a very conservative view of what was appropriate behaviour for middle-class women, the colleges sought to fill as much of their time and keep them under as much control as possible. The first students at Whitelands were faced with long terms and long days, limited contact with their family, a puritanical dress code and domestic duties as well as academic study. Making them sweep, wash and cook was regarded as an apprenticeship for taking charge of their own lives once they qualified and for instructing the families of those they taught. Southlands students woke at six and put out their gas lights at 10.20pm but the College authorities were more benign than elsewhere, considering their day was full enough without compelling them to carry out domestic chores. They were, however, expected to become proficient in domestic management.

Living conditions were often spartan – Southlands offered cold, unheated, partitioned cubicles, fronted by curtains, lit by gas, affording little privacy, with a bed, bolster, dressing chest, washstand and crockery. In 1877 there were just two bathrooms for more than a hundred girls. Yet these conditions were not unusual and often better than those students had left behind. Although the strictures against contact with men persisted until the end of the century, the College became more domesticated and students were given greater freedom, reflecting a more liberal approach by the Wesleyan

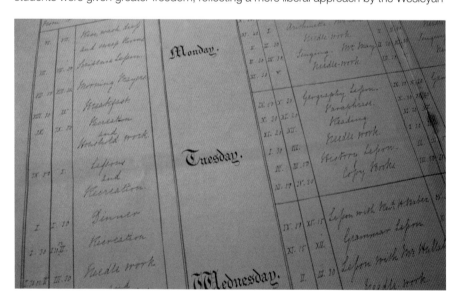

Below: A student's impression of May Day at Whitelands, 1889.

Bottom: May Queen bookplate signed by the Principal and John Ruskin in which the recipient is congratulated for 'never being ashamed to admit she is wrong'.

church towards women. The girls were given a free afternoon every Thursday which allowed them to explore London while evenings were given over to private study, albeit supervised. They were also encouraged to take up sport, including hockey, rowing and swimming. A similar pattern emerged among most of the women's training colleges during the 1890s, often through pressure from students, as petty rules were removed, domestic duties abandoned, dress codes relaxed and free time cultivated. Students were beginning to be treated as young women, boosting their self-confidence.

Whitelands regarded itself as the pre-eminent women's training college, a reputation bolstered by the May Day festival which began in 1881. This arose out of links between the College and John Ruskin, dating from 1877, which also led Edward Burne-Jones to design a series of outstanding stained glass windows for the College chapel, executed by William Morris. Ruskin had been seeking a vehicle for the revival of this pagan festival, and in Whitelands found an Anglican college willing to do so. Ruskin's own views of women's role in society, which emphasized their separateness and femininity, were becoming increasingly quaint, but the festival was a huge success and the College benefited from its association with the many distinguished women who came to the College every year to invest the new May Queen.

Close cohabitation and a relatively cloistered existence bred a strong bond between many of the students for theirs was a lonely social existence after they qualified. While the best students often had their pick of headships at schools up and down the country – and often exported their teaching skills to schools and training colleges in British colonies around the globe – they were a class apart from both those they taught and those who employed them. Elementary school teaching was also regarded as inferior to teaching in the new secondary schools. Newly qualified teachers emerging from the colleges were often resented by the many unqualified staff still teaching in the schools they joined. It was not surprising that many former students wished to keep in touch with each other. Annual reunions started at Whitelands in 1875 and a former students' association, the Guild of St Ursula, was established in 1878. Well-attended annual reunions were held at

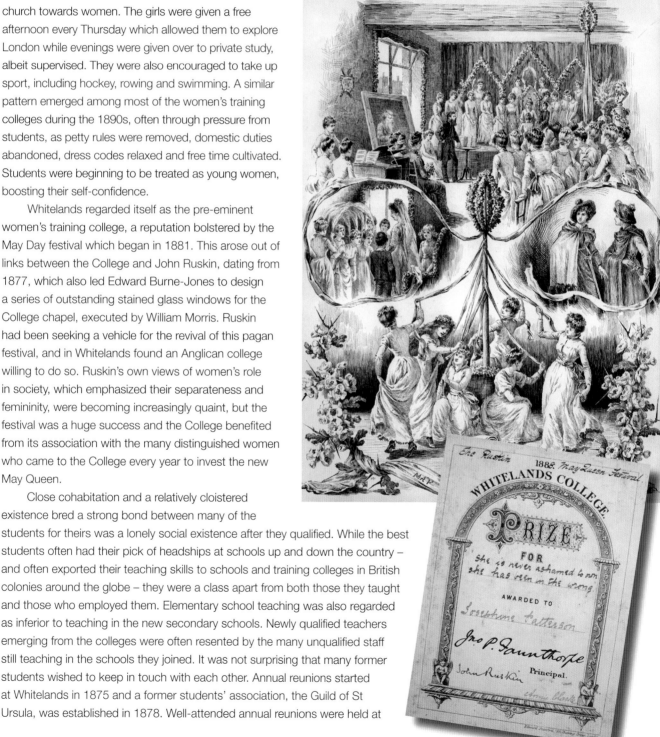

Stained glass windows designed by Edward Burne-Jones and produced by William Morris for the Whitelands chapel in Chelsea. The first window of St Ursula was paid for by the Seniors of 1882. By 1893 the chapel had windows depicting 12 female saints.

Southlands from the 1880s, and there were monthly meetings for those girls who had qualified at Wandsworth.

By 1900 all four voluntary colleges were well established. By supplying qualified teachers for voluntary and state elementary schools, they had become valued partners of the state. They were helping their founding bodies, whether the three churches or the exponents of the philosophy of Friedrich Froebel, to maintain a degree of influence within the national education system. And by offering capable young women the chance for personal fulfilment through a professional qualification when such opportunities remained rare, they were making an important contribution towards the growing role of women in society.

STRUGGLE FOR RECOGNITION
1900–1944

The growing confidence of women in fighting for greater freedom and independence was reflected in the women's training colleges. Under a succession of strong-minded, charismatic and passionate women as Principals, the colleges gradually broke free of the constraints imposed upon them by a male-dominated view of female propriety. They embraced a wider view of the world, in part through more freedom for their students, as they pursued their goal of creating a liberal teaching profession which would transform the way young children were taught. Achieving this ambition was often difficult. The teachers they sent out into the country's schools continued to find resistance to new ways of doing things. After the First World War, economic circumstances interrupted expansion yet all four colleges moved to larger premises. Responsibility was transferred to the universities for teacher training but they proved hostile to the ideal of a graduate profession for elementary school teachers. And the need to evacuate the colleges from London during the Second World War caused major disruption to their communal life.

Above: St Charles' College, North Kensington, 1905.

Opposite: Froebel students making dolls' houses.

The number of student teachers rose from 4,000 in 1890 to 13,000 in 1914. From 1907 those intending to train as teachers were encouraged by the payment of grants to stay on at the new secondary schools until they were 17 or 18. The effect was to channel most aspirants to the training colleges, reducing the number of pupil-teachers to just 1,500 by 1911. More training colleges were opened as the number of those wishing to train as teachers increased. Most of them were provided by the new local education authorities but there were also more voluntary training colleges, including six new Catholic colleges opened between 1903 and 1910.

As in the past, the voluntary colleges faced the opportunity to expand based on increased numbers of students as well as the challenge of competition from the new training colleges. The pressure to keep up was perhaps felt most keenly at Wandsworth. Here the key influence was Mother Janet Stuart whose whole approach to education was characterized by concern for the individual. The College's historian, Eileen Foster, has written that Stuart 'never ceased to encourage the students in their chosen vocation, and spoke of the influence they would have, not only on the children whom they taught, but also on the children's families'. One of the main challenges she faced was improving the quality of teaching. After 1904 all new lay staff and almost all religious appointed to teach came to the College with appropriate qualifications while several of the nuns already teaching studied for external degrees. The College premises in Wandsworth were now too small and a new property was acquired in St Charles' Square, North Kensington. In January 1905 the College reopened with 99 students as St Charles' College.

Above: Scene from *Twelfth Night* and programme, 1910.

Left: Whitelands hockey team, 1912–13.

JANET STUART

Janet Stuart was born in Cottesmore in Rutland in 1857, the youngest of the 12 children of an Anglican rector. Converting to Catholicism at the age of 22, she joined the Society of the Sacred Heart at Roehampton in 1882. She became deeply interested in education and developed a child-centred view of education which was ahead of its time. Writing several works on educational philosophy and practice, she believed that the personal character of the teacher was of critical importance, since children were heavily influenced by those who taught them. She was also an advocate of improving the calibre of teachers through professional qualifications. Elected Superior General of the Society in 1911, she died in 1914.

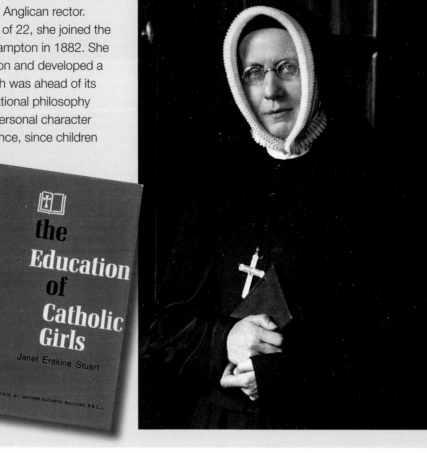

the Education of Catholic Girls

Janet Erskine Stuart

WITH A PREFACE BY MOTHER KATHRYN SULLIVAN, R.S.C.J.

Far right: Mother Janet Stuart.

Right: *The Education of Catholic Girls,* written by Stuart.

At Froebel, Esther Lawrence was appointed Principal in 1901. The College historian, Peter Weston, wrote that she 'combined vision and practical determination to an unusual degree'. She understood that the Froebel philosophy would remain relevant only if it took into account modern educational developments. She initiated a process of renewal which has been repeated regularly ever since. She was also eager to pursue that elusive goal of raising the status of the elementary school teacher but the College's application to become a school of the University of London in 1902 was disdainfully rejected. She strove hard to bridge the gap between training college and university, subsidizing at least one student to spend a few terms as a Home Student at Oxford for the sheer intellectual and social enjoyment of it. As for her students at Froebel, she encouraged the formation of numerous clubs and societies, which became a common feature at most training colleges. She also maintained Froebel's non-denominational ethos, with College assemblies reflecting a wide range of religious views. Many Froebel students still went on to teach in private schools, unlike their peers at other colleges. Those who opted for state schools often found the experience dispiriting – as one student put it in 1910, teaching a class of 60 in an elementary school in Clerkenwell, 'we have to think in batches and not in individuals'. It was this approach to teaching which Froebel and the other colleges were still seeking to change.

Clara Luard became the first woman Principal of Whitelands in 1907. She met the challenge of competition by reforming the curriculum over which colleges had been given greater flexibility through regulations issued in 1901. The course she devised in 1911, providing a sound general education in the first year and professional training in theory and practice in the second, was widely copied. She overhauled the way the College was run, with the head governess becoming Vice-Principal and governesses becoming lecturers. She reinvigorated the teaching staff by appointing lecturers with external experience. She also pressed for the appointment of women to the governing body although this only occurred after pressure from the Board of Education in 1914. Like Miss Lawrence at Froebel, Miss Luard ensured the College remained attractive to intending students, given the increased choice of colleges they were now given. She improved living conditions, relaxed discipline and encouraged students to form clubs and societies. Sport, already fostered at other colleges, was boosted by the creation of a games club in 1907, offering hockey, tennis, swimming, netball and croquet. The College was already recruiting day students, who formed around ten per cent of the total of some 200.

The pattern of change was similar at Southlands. Although a female Principal was not appointed until 1914, alterations in the curriculum were made under a senior member of staff, Miss Walker. One of these was the introduction of psychology, with lectures given by the first Professor of Education at University College, London. Another innovation was sending language specialists abroad for a year. To overcome the criticism that teaching practice did little to prepare those heading for smaller, rural schools, the College sent students to a group of schools in the Surrey countryside

Students with the donkey that was kept in the garden at St Charles' Square in Kensington.

Above: Page from student nature album.

Below: Seniors' picnic, 1926.

from 1910. As elsewhere, students were encouraged to take more exercise. Hockey, swimming and dancing were introduced, although the latter was viewed by the governing body with some suspicion.

The training colleges made their own contribution towards the national service performed by women during the First World War. With a third of students at men's training colleges joining up within weeks of the war breaking out, the women's colleges supplied the teachers needed to fill the places previously taken by men. With shortages of male staff in some secondary schools, women trained as elementary teachers were often asked to step in. It was service like this which eventually persuaded the men in parliament to give women the vote, initially in 1918 only to those over 30, extended ten years later to all women over 21.

The war, however, put paid to any idea of relocating Whitelands which, like Froebel and Southlands, was becoming overcrowded. For all three colleges, removal to more spacious accommodation became central to their post-war plans.

After the war the Education Act of 1918 gave a further fillip to the colleges by raising the school leaving age to 14 and abolishing fees for elementary schools. With pensions and national pay scales, the profession was becoming more attractive for women. It seemed as if the colleges were about to embark on a period of prosperous expansion. The volatile economic situation of the inter-war years put an end to such dreams. Harsh spending cuts fell on the education budget in 1922. One Froebel student recalled that a third of her peers left College without jobs. As local education authorities struggled to make economies, many of them adopted a bar on the employment of married women teachers, which was eased only in the mid-1930s and eventually banned altogether by the 1944 Education Act.

From 1925 the Board of Education gradually transferred responsibility for examining the teaching certificate to the universities. A minimum entry standard, based on the School Certificate, the predecessor of GCSEs, was introduced. The four training colleges were linked with colleges of the University of London which formed a Training College Delegacy in 1928 – Froebel and St Charles' with Bedford College, Southlands with Birkbeck and Whitelands with King's College. Although inspections carried out for the Delegacy revealed that the colleges still maintained an overcrowded curriculum, the inspectors found that they were achieving creditable academic results. In 1931 almost half of all students were gaining A and B grades, while almost all of them were obtaining A–C grades.

This was the fruit borne of the hard work done by the colleges to make improvements even before the University Delegacy had been formed. Results were also helped

The "W.B.C"

by rising applications which enabled the colleges to be more selective. In 1925, for instance, Southlands had 600 applications when the College population was just 148, most of whom were following a two-year course. Numbers increased at all the colleges – Whitelands reached a peak of 241 during the 1920s, St Charles', the smallest of them all, grew to 121 in 1926, Froebel was teaching 252 in 1928, and Southlands hit a new high of 168 in 1931.

At Whitelands, Winifred Mercier, who became Principal in 1918, was heavily involved in professional bodies outside the College, helping to overhaul the content and form of professional syllabuses and examinations. She further broadened the horizons of her students, arranging public lectures at the College, sending students on fieldwork and arranging exchanges with other training colleges. She persuaded the College Council to grant staff a sabbatical term for travel or study after seven years' service. She was also

Above and top: Student's notes on beekeeping and tending beehives at Battersea, 1926.

able to add a third year to the course for all students, who were funded by scholarships endowed by the College. Similar changes were made by Miss Brunyate, the Principal of Southlands from 1918 until 1931. She liberalized the regime, turning cubicles into study bedrooms and permitting students to visit London unsupervised in pairs. Field work was introduced in 1923 as were visits abroad, to Switzerland and Belgium. It was during this period that a number of students completed degrees alongside their certificates, several of them winning firsts.

Manresa Hall, a former Jesuit chapel with magnificent domed ceilings, arches and pillars at Whitelands College.

GROVE HOUSE

Grove House, the home of Froebel College, stands on the site of Roehampton House, built by Sir Richard Weston, later the Earl of Portland, around 1628. The chapel was consecrated by Archbishop Laud and the guests at the house included the King, Charles I, and his queen, Henrietta Maria. Weston died heavily in debt and the estate was sold in parcels, with the dowager Countess of Devonshire acquiring the house in 1650. Passing through several different owners, Roehampton House was demolished in 1786 by Sir Joshua Vanneck. The present building was built in the early 1790s to a design by the renowned architect James Wyatt. Once again the house was owned by a number of different families until it was acquired by the Lyne Stephens family in 1843, in whose possession the house remained until 1912. The family mausoleum still stands in the grounds and is still owned by the family. The house was bought by the sitting tenant, an American, Charles Fischer, who is said to have built the cascade in the grounds to drown out the sound of the bells from the convent of the Society of the Sacred Heart close by. His sudden disappearance, indebted to the Lyne Stephens family, led to the latter family resuming ownership. During the First World War the house was occupied by the Royal Flying Corps. In poor condition, Grove House was put on the market in 1919, and was bought by Claude Montefiore, Chairman of the Froebel Educational Institute, for £29,750 in August 1921.

The main reception, Grove House, 1920s.

Claude Montefiore with Froebel staff. Esther Lawrence is on Montefiore's right.

At Froebel Miss Lawrence was always clear that the College had two purposes – firstly, vocational, and secondly, as a preparation for life beyond the schoolroom. She also succeeded in extending the training course to three years from 1920, funded partly by grants made to students by the Board of Education. Given the strict traditions of the Catholic church, change came less readily at St Charles'. Although Mother Edith Monahan relaxed the oppressive disciplinary regime when she became Principal in 1925, it would not be until the arrival of Mother Eileen Fincham in 1936 that more changes were made.

The post-war growth of the colleges added to the pressure experienced at Froebel, Whitelands and Southlands because of overcrowded and unsatisfactory premises. In 1921 Grove House, a run-down but substantial property surrounded by spacious gardens, adjacent to the convent of the Society of the Sacred Heart in Roehampton, was acquired on behalf of Froebel by Claude Montefiore. A wealthy

Below: Eurhythmics by the lake at Grove House in the 1920s.

Below left: Student's field work album.

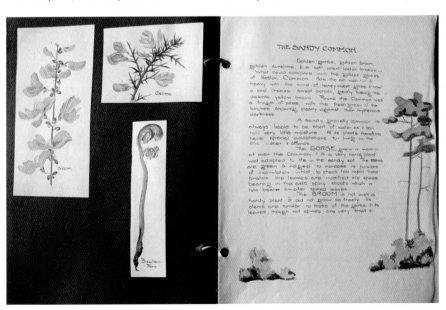

Right: Southlands badge.

Below: Froebel students in the gardens of Grove House.

philanthropist, who was also secretary of the Froebel Society, he was a key benefactor of the College until his death in 1938. Following refurbishment, renovation and improvements, Grove House became the home of the College in January 1922, with 115 resident students and 70 day students. Miss Lawrence, having apparently used the move as an opportunity to abolish all the College rules, had to reconsider when she discovered her students were entertaining young gentlemen to tea and even supper in their rooms. The buildings were constantly adapted and improved, while new ones were added, such as a block for zoology and botany in 1923.

At Southlands, a much needed alternative site, Belmont, in Wimbledon, was acquired in 1927. Delays in preparing the property following the sale of the College's Battersea premises forced the College to decamp to distant Dover, where it occupied the Burlington Hotel until 1929. In Wimbledon single study bedrooms were provided in three new blocks, a major improvement. The only omission was a chapel for which the student society started raising funds but whose construction was deferred because of the depression and then another world war.

Winifred Mercier began a development fund for new College buildings at Whitelands in the mid-1920s. Sites in Roehampton were discounted because of their proximity to Froebel, an indication of the distant relationship between the colleges. Instead, a 12-acre site was acquired at Melrose Gardens in East

Putney. Miss Mercier's ambition was obvious from the appointment of the eminent architect, Sir Giles Gilbert Scott, to design the new buildings. Work began in December 1928 and the buildings were opened by Queen Mary (who six years earlier had visited Froebel just after Grove House had been opened) in June 1931. The new College boasted the largest volume of parquet flooring in any building in Europe. Each study bedroom was equipped with a suite of matching oak furniture and fittings while the surround of every fireplace was created from Delft tiles. The only separate building was the chapel, for which students past and present had raised funds, and to which were transferred the stained glass Burne-Jones windows from the old chapel. The whole complex was an ambitious statement of the value and importance of the College. It was Miss Mercier's supreme achievement. She retired three years later, already terminally ill, dying just months after stepping down. She was succeeded by Dorothy Counsell, her Vice-Principal. By then, all the colleges were suffering from the ravages of the world depression. The state funded fewer training

Above: Whitelands moved to Melrose Gardens in East Putney in 1931.

Below: Queen Mary, with Winifred Mercier on her right, at the opening of the new Whitelands' buildings designed by Sir Giles Gilbert Scott, 1931.

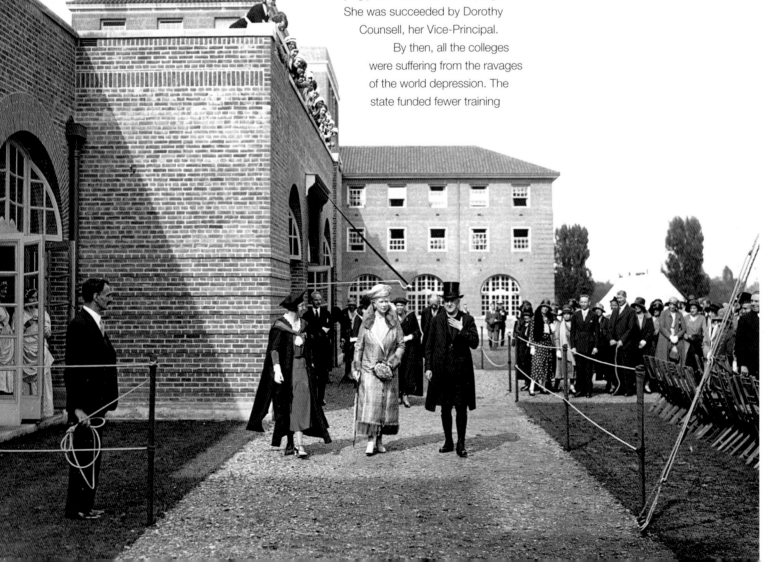

Above: Eglantyne Jebb who succeeded Esther Lawrence at Froebel.

Below: Preparing for finals at St Charles' College, 1938.

places and, for those who qualified, there were fewer jobs. Froebel was badly hit for it sent a much larger proportion of its students to private schools and so lacked the scope to make up from the private sector the deficiency in places funded by the state.

This was a route that could be pursued by the other colleges, which also sought to attract overseas students, especially from those parts of the world where their churches were involved in missionary activity. St Charles' started a course for those teaching in overseas missions. At Southlands, where numbers dropped to 124 in 1934, an overseas course was introduced in the same year and a group of Indian students studied at the College each year until 1939. To bring in much needed income, the College rented out bedrooms to young teachers, librarians and musicians. At St Charles', the entrance fees paid by students were increased to make up for a reduction in state aid, creating a problem for poor families. Closure was not unthinkable. Whitelands survived thanks only to a generous gift from the industrialist Lord Nuffield which paid off the College's overdraft, while the closure of three other Anglican training colleges enabled Whitelands to increase its intake. St Charles' too could not have continued without the support of the Society of the Sacred Heart nor Froebel without the support of Claude Montefiore.

It was not a time for educational innovation or reform. Although the Hadow Report on education in 1933 endorsed the Froebel approach to infant and nursery education, resources were too scarce to implement any changes. Nevertheless, a new generation of Principals did what they could to maintain momentum within the colleges. By the end of the 1930s Dorothy Counsell at Whitelands had been able to allow almost all teaching staff to concentrate on their specialist subjects. St Charles' at last began to catch up with the other colleges when Mother Eileen Fincham became Principal in 1936. She brought a new vision to the College from her experience over 18 years as Principal of the Society's northern training college at Fenham in Newcastle. She immediately abolished the rule of silence and the College uniform, which had long since disappeared from other training colleges. The other long overdue changes she made included the creation of study bedrooms, the addition of a new library and common room, the creation of clubs and societies and the liberation of students from a repressive timetable. Eglantyne Jebb, whose cousin of the same name founded the organization now known as Save the Children, succeeded Esther Lawrence at Froebel. One of her first decisions was to reform the College syllabus so that students were involved directly with children from their first term. Given the support of the Hadow Report, she was also eager for more Froebel-trained teachers to work in state schools. One former student recalled how 'Miss Jebb inspired a very able and dedicated staff to promote an invasion of such teachers into the state system'. The same student also remembered how difficult this was for Froebel teachers. One of her first posts was teaching a class of 60 six-year-olds in an elementary school in Liverpool where the head rejected anything other than reading, writing and arithmetic as 'Froebel Frills'.

Left: Froebel students were relocated to Knebworth House during the war.

Below: Student bedroom at Knebworth House.

Bottom: Elm Grove and the main chapel were severely damaged in 1940.

The Second World War once again highlighted the national importance of teaching as so many men and women left the profession for war service. Repeating the contribution the colleges had made in an earlier conflict was more difficult a second time around. Both teaching practice and pupil education were disrupted. All four colleges were compelled to leave London because of the threat from bombing. In 1939 Froebel let Grove House to the National Provincial Bank and moved to Knebworth House, with first-year students occupying nearby Offley Place. St Charles' took refuge with the convent of St Gabriel's at Cold Ash in Berkshire. Grove House suffered bomb damage during the summer of 1940 while the North Kensington property occupied by St Charles' was bombed four times during 1941. Southlands, considered safe enough in Wimbledon during the first year of the war, moved out in 1940, heading for the Methodist Holiday Home, Highbury, in Weston-super-Mare. Belmont was given over to the army. Whitelands perhaps endured the most disruption. An original plan to move to Wales proved abortive so the College was given permission to remain for the time being in Putney. The onset of the Blitz (the College was damaged by incendiary bombs during a raid in February 1941) prevented the return of many students. To overcome this problem, a correspondence course was introduced, coupled with teaching practice in local schools. Students were split between a school in Halifax and Homerton College in Cambridge, which stretched the College's finances and did little for its community life. One writer in the College magazine suggested that the College's motto should have been 'Join Whitelands and see England'. The Putney property became home to several hundred refugees from Gibraltar. Miss Counsell insisted that all students gathered in Cambridge in the summer of 1941 to

Nuns from the Convent of the Sacred Heart at Roehampton taking part in the war effort.

celebrate the College centenary and the May Queen festival, which continued throughout the war, albeit on a less elaborate scale. That autumn it was possible for the entire College to be rehoused in Bede College, Durham. Here, as one student later recalled, the Whitelands girls, perhaps contrary to their own perception, 'were a revelation to the cloistered girls and Principals of the local Durham colleges'. They threw themselves with gusto into university life, enjoying the company of young men, taking part in clubs and societies. For many of them, it was a transforming experience.

Wartime thinking would also transform the post-war educational world. As the intentions of the government became clearer, they were warmly welcomed by Dorothy Counsell, the Principal of Whitelands, who foresaw the growing demand for teachers. It was an initiative which would have a fundamental impact on all four colleges.

TRAINING MORE TEACHERS
1944–1970

The 1944 Education Act set out the pattern for education in England and Wales for the next four decades. Since it relied for its implementation on a growing number of qualified teachers, the state took an increasing interest in teacher training. As the country recovered from the war and returned to prosperity, the state's plans for education became more ambitious. With a massive expansion of teacher training, the four colleges admitted more students, including men, expanded their courses, which included the introduction of a degree in education, and added to their buildings and facilities. This was accompanied by social change which led to a fundamental shift in the relationship between the colleges and their students, influenced in particular by the lowering of the age of majority to 18.

Above: Science at Digby Stuart, 1947.

Opposite: Froebel College is situated within four acres of beautiful heritage gardens, which include a picturesque lake and a 'faux' bridge, known as the Froebel Folly.

The catalyst for changes in teacher training was the McNair Report of 1944. It criticized a fragmented and incoherent system made up of too many small colleges. Of the 83 training colleges, 60 were women's colleges and 64 had fewer than 150 students, including Southlands and the College run by the Society of the Sacred Heart, renamed Digby Stuart College after the war. Voluntary colleges numbered 54 and the total number of students in training at any one time was just 10,000.

One of the Report's main recommendations was the creation of a three-year training course, offered by Froebel and Whitelands to a limited number of students for some years, but this was not introduced until 1960. In the interim period only Froebel secured a concession allowing the College to maintain its own three-year course.

McNair gave an enhanced role to the universities in supervising the training colleges. The four colleges became the responsibility of the University of London Institute of Education (ULIE), formed in 1949 as the area training organization for the London area. ULIE monitored the curriculum, kept an eye on college property and administration, and approved all new staff appointments. The relationship between the two sides was variable. The fiercely independent colleges were suspicious of anything which might infringe their autonomy and felt that ULIE staff, whose expertise mainly lay in secondary education, lacked a proper understanding of primary schooling.

Above: Southlands teaching practice, late 1950s.

Left: 'A child's play is his work' – Friedrich Froebel placed great emphasis on the role of art in developing children's symbolic understandings, creativity and self-expression.

Top: Southlands College was located in Wimbledon from 1930 to 1997. This watercolour by Elizabeth Peace was painted in 1996 shortly before Southlands moved to its new site in Roehampton.

Above: Nissen huts left in the grounds of Southlands after the war were used until new buildings were constructed.

As the historian of Whitelands later recorded, 'the University of London sought to extend its influence over the training colleges it had recently absorbed, but at Whitelands the policy was to maintain its own traditional standards as being in the best interests of the teaching profession'. The disenchantment of the colleges was ultimately shared by the Ministry of Education which, when planning for major expansion of teacher training in the late 1950s, decided to communicate directly with the colleges. On the other hand, as the historian of Froebel College noted, the objectivity of the ULIE could be helpful. The College made changes both to its curriculum and to the way teaching practice was organized following an inspection by the ULIE in the late 1940s. The influence of the ULIE also helped to standardize the curriculum throughout the colleges.

All these changes were under way as the colleges arrived back in London after the end of the war. Whitelands and Froebel returned from exile in July 1945. The Whitelands buildings in Putney were badly in need

of repair but in spite of this there were nearly 250 students on the roll within a year. At Froebel, where Grove House was badly in need of remedial work, the College reopened with 284 students, including 35 day students. In January 1946 Southlands started again in Wimbledon although it had to retain a base in Weston-super-Mare until 1950, since the buildings in London could no longer accommodate the extra number of students. With Britain impoverished after the war, it was four years before additional accommodation was provided, although a nearby former boys' school, Beltane, was acquired in 1946, bringing with it more land for playing fields. The Society of the Sacred Heart did not move its training college back to North Kensington. Acute bomb damage, coupled with the decline of the local area and a desire among those who had been evacuated to Berkshire for a more tranquil situation on their return to London, led the Society to relocate the College alongside the convent in Roehampton. This too had been severely damaged during the war. The chapel had been completely destroyed and was rebuilt only in 1960. Repair work delayed the return of the 105 students until October 1946 when the College was renamed Digby Stuart.

While Britain was still paying for the war, change came slowly. It must have been irksome for those students taking up places at Froebel in the late 1940s to find that visits from men were still limited, signing out of college was still insisted upon and wirelesses were not allowed in the first year. 'Moral lapses', reflected one student from the mid-1950s, 'were treated very strictly. An unmarried student in our year was asked to leave when she became pregnant.' As another student noted, 'the "young lady" ethos was pretty strong still'. Yet, according to one student, the regime was relatively liberal compared with that still in force elsewhere. At Whitelands, where the ten o'clock evening curfew was signalled by the ringing of the angelus, a minimum of rules was accompanied by high expectations of behaviour. As one student later remembered, 'staff and the College trusted us in all areas, even to allowing men in our rooms until 9pm. [This was] unheard of in other colleges'. The social background of students at both colleges was largely unchanged. Mainly middle class with a handful from the working class, they ranged from girls from a co-educational grammar school in a Welsh mining town to those whose public schools rather frowned on training colleges but for whom, having failed to enter university, 'the cachet of going to one of the best teacher-training colleges rescued them from actual shame'. For both types, though, the training colleges offered higher education opportunities otherwise still scarce. They also instilled long-lasting ideals in their students. One remembered how 'the teaching approach of tolerance and understanding made a very deep impression … I left college with high ideals and the belief that teachers could influence the next generation and make the world a better place'. Recruitment was buoyant. At Froebel, there were 200 applicants for 80 places in 1949, while Digby Stuart was able to admit 100 students every year from the early 1950s.

Below: Gymnasts from the United States practising in the grounds of Southlands College. The College provided accommodation for women athletes competing in the Olympics Games of 1948.

Above: Digby Stuart group attending an exhibition at Olympia in 1956.

Far right: John Ruskin's May Day cross.

The colleges began developing new courses to prepare students for infant and secondary schools as well as junior schools. By the mid-1950s both Whitelands and Southlands were training students as secondary teachers, usually for entry into the secondary modern schools rather than the grammar schools, where graduates were preferred.

In 1960 a three-year course finally became standard at all training colleges. The government was eager to encourage a significant increase in qualified teachers to meet the forecast rise in the school population. This expansion was to be met largely by the state sector. Colleges run by local education authorities had accounted for only 29 of the 83 colleges in existence in 1945. By 1968, although the number of voluntary colleges was almost the same, at 53, local education authority colleges had risen to 113. Nevertheless, the voluntary colleges were also asked to take their fair share of the rising volume of trainee teachers. Whitelands had already grown to 445 students by 1961. Student numbers at Digby Stuart, previously the smallest of the four colleges, soared to 500 by 1962. This expansion was reinforced by the Robbins Report in 1962 which urged a substantial growth in higher education. More particularly, Robbins recommended the transformation of the training colleges into colleges of education and the introduction of the Bachelor of Education degree for intending teachers. By 1969, there were 671 students at Froebel and well over 800 each at Digby Stuart, Whitelands and Southlands. Once again the colleges were beginning to suffer from a lack of space. Since a limited building programme could not meet the demand for more residential places, the majority of students in most of the colleges quickly became non-resident. By 1965, for example, there were already 224 day students at Whitelands.

All four colleges also began admitting men. When the first 12 male students joined Froebel in 1967, one female student later remembered how they seemed to go around in pairs 'looking hunted'. In 1969 the largest number was to be found at Southlands, with 161 men compared with 674 women. There were 84 at Whitelands and 46 at Froebel with, understandably, just six at Digby Stuart.

With the admission of men, militancy at the colleges increased since they took over most of the positions within the student unions. There had been mounting pressure for some time from national student bodies for a more relaxed approach to discipline and for greater scope for students to run their own affairs. Opinion was also growing in favour of lowering the age of majority from 21 to 18. This took effect in January 1970 when college authorities were relieved of their quasi-parental responsibilities. But the four colleges never experienced the extreme militancy which affected colleges and universities elsewhere during the late 1960s. At Whitelands, the Principal, Molly Saunders, wrote in 1968 that

'at a time when student unrest makes news, it is good to know that the students here have shown a marked sense of responsibility in running their own affairs and in their contribution to the college as a whole'. And the College authorities were willing to move with the spirit of the times. At Southlands, students won places on the College governing body by 1968. In the following year the College agreed that the presidency of the student union should become a sabbatical post. College rules were liberalized; visiting hours were no longer regulated by a bell and the dress code for attending lectures was abolished. On the other hand, attempts by students to introduce alcohol were consistently refused. The pattern was similar in the other colleges. At Digby Stuart, for instance, under Sister Dorothy Bell, who became Principal in 1969, mixed visiting was initiated in the same year and student representatives joined the governing body and academic board.

Digby Stuart also tackled the issue of a student community which was no longer exclusively Catholic. This affected other colleges – at Southlands only some 40 per cent of students were Methodist by the early 1970s – but it was perhaps felt most acutely at Digby Stuart, where the liberalization begun so recently by Pope John XXIII was not universally accepted. But Sister Dorothy, strong-minded and persuasive, was happy to encourage the creation of what Eileen Foster, the College's historian, described as 'a more open Christian community where those of all denominations had the opportunity to explore the beliefs which linked them rather than those which separated them'.

The arrival of male students also began to influence college appointments. Gradually more and more women would make way for men, a reversion to the situation which had occurred in the earliest days of the colleges. In 1970 Roy Knight became the first male Principal of Whitelands since John Faunthorpe's resignation in 1907. At Froebel, where there had been 30 single women on the teaching staff of 35 in 1958, 29 of the 66 staff in 1971 were men, while 16 of the 37 women were married.

The student body began to alter in other ways. Mature and part-time students appeared for the first time. Although small in number – there were 48 at Whitelands in 1966 – they made quite an impact on those around them. One student at the College in the early 1970s later wrote how 'the mature students were the ones who seemed to push the boundaries more than school leavers'. Mature students had a different perspective. One of the first to attend Whitelands, a 43-year-old former nurse, felt quite isolated from her fellow students, although she always felt secure, happy and accepted.

Roy Knight became the Principal of Whitelands in 1970.

Below: Laying the foundation stone for the Student Union at Southlands, Wimbledon, 1967.

Bottom: The Chapel of the Sacred Heart at Digby Stuart College.

The national three-year training course brought an end to the award of the National Froebel Foundation certificates at Froebel College. Southlands became the first of the colleges to add the Postgraduate Certificate of Education (PGCE) in 1960, offering teacher training in primary and secondary education to graduates. At the same time the College also offered a general degree course in philosophy, theology and ethics. The new Bachelor of Education (BEd) degree was first introduced by Whitelands in 1965. The BEd consisted of the Certificate of Education course, followed by a fourth year focused on academic work. In general this was taken up only by around ten per cent of students. In all the colleges the curriculum became much wider. At Whitelands the curriculum swelled to embrace a choice of 14 main subjects in addition to the theory and practice of education. Froebel introduced a diploma in the teaching of music and a research project on pre-school programmes for disadvantaged children. Southlands offered specialist courses in youth work, comparative education and special needs education, as well as short courses in business and commerce, refresher courses for practising teachers, and courses aimed at the education of ethnic minority students.

Sister Dorothy Bell, the Principal of Digby Stuart, remembered the conversation she had with her predecessor, the redoubtable Sister Mary Richardson, as they had strolled down the College garden. Sister Mary, who had presided over considerable change since her appointment in 1949, mused to her successor that there would be even greater change, so much so that she believed that the College would eventually be educating young people not just to become teachers, but to join other professions, such as social work and psychology. Here, more than 30 years before the event, was an early vision of a university at Roehampton. Yet nothing could have seemed further away when in June 1970 the Department for Education and Science (DES) announced that a declining birth rate meant that the rapid expansion of colleges during the previous decade would now be thrown into reverse.

THE ROEHAMPTON INSTITUTE OF HIGHER EDUCATION

PART 2

CREATING THE INSTITUTE
1970–1980

Suddenly, after a long period of sustained growth, the four colleges faced a battle for survival as savage cuts were made to teacher-training places. Colleges all over the country were closed down during the 1970s. The future of the colleges was secured only through a hastily arranged and officially encouraged alliance, bringing them into a close relationship for the first time in their history. The outcome was the Roehampton Institute of Higher Education which aimed to make up for the reduced number of trainee teachers by offering non-teaching degrees validated by the University of London. While there were inevitable tensions among this group of proudly independent bodies, the process of transforming them into a single unified organization under the Institute's first Rector, Kevin Keohane, was well under way by the end of the decade.

Above: Kevin Keohane CBE became the first Rector of the new federation of colleges in 1976. He was an inspiring leader with endless patience, boundless optimism and a talent for being both tough and kind-hearted. On his retirement, after 12 years, Keohane left behind a flourishing institution.

Opposite: Student demonstration, 1971.

Previous spread: The Wisteria Walk at Grove House.

The government's announcement in the summer of 1970 was followed in the next year by the publication of the James Report, which had enquired into teacher education and training. This heralded the end of the system of training teachers which had been developed over the previous century or more. Lord James, Vice-Chancellor of York University, still saw a future for a dedicated teacher-training sector but placed much more emphasis on in-service training.

In describing the period from the early 1970s to the early 1980s, the historian of the University of London Institute of Education (ULIE) wrote that 'political and public hostility, financial stringency, ideological controversies, student militancy, redundancies and low morale among staff characterized the teacher education world of this period'. For the Principals of the four colleges, no more warning of a turbulent future was needed than the message of the meeting at a college of education outside Oxford to which the heads of all such colleges had been invited. There, Sister Dorothy Bell recalled, they were told by the Secretary of State, Margaret Thatcher, that cuts were being planned.

The relevant minister at the time had already decided that two of the four voluntary colleges would have to close, the DES having declared that any training colleges in south-west London with fewer than 2,000 students would not be viable. But Pauline Perry, then Staff Inspector for Teacher Training in Her Majesty's Inspectorate, believed there was an alternative to closure. She was aware of the strengths of the individual colleges and the contribution they had made to teacher training. She asked the minister to consider their merger while reducing by half their teacher-training places. The minister's reluctance was shared by the senior civil servant

Early RIHE prospectuses.

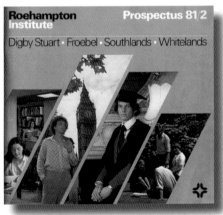

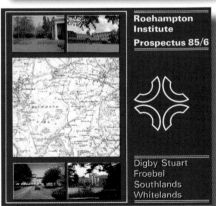

Above: Choosing books in the Digby Stuart Library.

Right: Whitelands students at work, 1976.

at the DES, Hugh Harding, known to his colleagues as 'Hush Puppy Hugh', but the minister, with some reservations, finally agreed.

Although the government was planning to expand higher education at the same time as it was cutting back on teacher training, the idea of meeting this expansion in part by using spare capacity in the colleges of education came about fortuitously. The same DES committee was considering both policies and, at one meeting, it suddenly struck the respective civil servants with responsibility for higher education and teacher training that the surplus training places could be filled by students following non-education degrees, using specialist subject teachers already employed in the colleges. The idea was enthusiastically supported by Hugh Harding and set out in the government White Paper issued in December 1972, entitled 'Education: A Framework for Expansion'. The implications for teacher training were certainly bleak, with a planned reduction in places from 114,000 in 1972 to 70,000 in 1981. The White Paper also advocated using the colleges to expand higher education outside the universities. These ideas were presented in more detail in the DES circular published in March 1973. It made clear that the remaining teacher-training places would be more evenly distributed. This would have an even more severe impact on those areas over-provided with places like London, which faced a reduction of 40 per cent. The circular also

confirmed that the expansion of higher education places would make use of surplus teacher-training places. While the universities would continue to validate teacher-training courses, they would also play a key role in developing the diversification of courses in the colleges.

The four colleges, unaware that closing down two of their number had already been discussed, were nevertheless acutely conscious that their future depended on their cooperation after so many years of complete independence. They too were reaching the same conclusion as Pauline Perry. The DES had already encouraged them to consider combining. The four Principals, Dorothy Bell from Digby Stuart, Roy Knight from Whitelands, Pauline Callard from Southlands and Priscilla Steele from Froebel, met for the first time at Froebel on 28 June 1972. Previously they would perhaps have met once a year at the Senate House at the University of London. Those were the days, Dorothy Bell remembered, when 'you were the queen of your own domain'. That was no longer an option.

The Froebel meeting was just the first of many as the colleges struggled to find a mutually acceptable solution. Various options were discussed, including linking up with Chelsea College and with two nearby local authority colleges, Furzedown and Phillipa Fawcett. Roy Knight, the Principal of Whitelands, later set out what had been happening in the College magazine for 1973. He rehearsed the rationale for the colleges coming together. To meet government objectives, which involved cutting back on teacher training while increasing the quality of remaining provision and boosting the number of non-teacher-training higher education places, 'colleges

Above: Parkstead House, Whitelands, winter 2009.

Top left: Outside the Folk Club, Whitelands, 1978.

Above left: The Red Corridor, Whitelands, 1978.

are likely in the future to have to cooperate more closely in the courses they provide, either by direct amalgamation or by some vaguer pattern of association or federation'. During the past year, he wrote:

> There have been endless meetings of staff and governors, meetings with other colleges, meetings with ILEA, meetings within Church groupings, meetings with the University, and meetings with teachers and their associations. Gradually a pattern has emerged which we believe holds out the most exciting developments in the history of the College … We expect that the voluntary colleges of education in the Borough of Wandsworth – Whitelands (Anglican), Digby Stuart (Roman Catholic), Southlands (Methodist) and Froebel Institute (non-denominational) – will shortly work out a scheme of academic association to plan a common policy for courses and resources.

This would encompass traditional teacher training, in-service training and new multi-disciplinary degrees validated by ULIE. Each of the colleges, he insisted, would continue to recruit their own students and staff but students would draw on the combined resources of all the colleges.

Below: A glamorous prospectus shot, 1970s.

The four colleges were guided initially by the advice of Dr Eric Briault, the Education Officer for the Inner London Education Authority. At a meeting on 18 July 1973, Briault recommended the colleges should consider either the strongly centralized federation favoured by the DES or a looser association, allowing joint academic planning but also permitting considerable autonomy. The colleges had mixed views – Digby Stuart tended towards federation, Southlands towards association; Whitelands simply wished to ensure its future by belonging to the largest possible grouping and Froebel was still hoping for continued independence. Briault's final recommendation, produced in October 1973, came down in favour of a centralized federation which would have a viable population of some 3,000 students.

Under the chairmanship of William Taylor, Director of the ULIE, representatives of the four governing bodies met at Whitelands in early November and drew up a Statement of Intent. On 28 November 1973, 17 months after their first meeting, the Statement, committing the colleges to exploring the possibility of formal association, was signed by the chairmen of the four governing bodies and the four College Principals. A Formation Committee would be established, made up of the College Principals and two staff and two governors from each college. But in making this commitment, the Statement also expressed the wish that any constitution for the new federation should 'not be incompatible with the retention of the autonomy of the four colleges'. At Southlands, wrote Douglas Millbank in his history of the College for this period, 'fear was expressed lest federation should lead to eventual fusion'. It was a typical reaction. As Peter Weston pointed out in his history of Froebel, 'thus the struggle between centralization and college autonomy began, a struggle which would last indefinitely'. By 2010, however, integration and collaboration between the College Providing Bodies and the university had reached levels that not even the most optimistic of colleagues could have predicted at the time.

Roy Knight had also written how excited he was about 'the creation of an inter-denominational institution of Christian education'. Such an overtly faith-based conclusion was not much to the liking of several Froebel governors, including the chair of the governing body, Dame Joyce Bishop, as well as a number of staff. When the Formation Committee, which had met for the first time on 9 January 1974, gathered again at the end of the month, Dame Joyce announced that Froebel was still exploring other avenues to maintain its independence. One of these was the relocation of the College to Suffolk on the basis that Suffolk lacked a college of higher education. Dame Joyce was clutching at straws and nothing came from these alternative explorations. The failure of the Suffolk venture was popularly labelled 'Suffolk-ation' in the other colleges. Most Froebel staff recognized that collaboration was the only viable path for the College's survival.

Conversely, even before the Statement of Intent had been signed, the Catholic education authorities, in the shape of the Catholic Education Council (CEC), had also protested about an association, on the grounds that it would inevitably lead to amalgamation and thus the demise of a distinctive Catholic voice. There was more to this than appeared on the surface. Unlike the Church of England, which had sole control over the future of its own colleges, the control over the 16 Catholic colleges was split. Several were owned and operated by individual religious orders, like Digby Stuart, but others, including St Mary's, Strawberry Hill, were the responsibility of the CEC. Although a college planning group for all the Catholic colleges had been formed in 1973, the DES still saw the CEC as its main point of contact and the CEC began to believe that it should exercise the decision over which of the Catholic training colleges should close. The CEC saw Digby Stuart as a prime candidate for closure, mainly because it was seen as a rival for St Mary's.

A local school used for teaching practice preparing for a pet show.

A student room, 1978.

Even while Sister Dorothy Bell was working hard to help create the new institute, she was constantly fighting to persuade the Catholic education hierarchy that Digby Stuart should continue. It was only in April 1974, after the Formation Committee had been under way for several months, that the Catholic Bishops' Conference approved the College's continuing participation. There were constant objections from the CEC and several bishops queried why Digby Stuart should survive when they feared any federation would place the Catholic ethos of the College at risk. Although the Bishops' Conference ultimately gave strong support to the College at its meeting in late 1974, Digby Stuart's future was still being questioned as late as May 1975. Ultimately one of the arguments which proved most persuasive was the opportunity for working with other faiths which would arise from the creation of an ecumenical federation of colleges. The younger bishops in particular were supportive of Digby Stuart and Dorothy Bell also received strong backing from her governing body and from the Provincial of the Society of the Sacred Heart, Andrée Meylan. There was a price for Digby Stuart's survival – the closure of its sister college at Fenham in Newcastle.

The Statement of Intent allowed the colleges to enter into discussions with the DES about the way forward. The Department gave its general approval to the

Opposite: Students at the Digby Stuart 'Going Down' dinner, 1979.

proposals in February 1974. At the time the country was going to the polls in the middle of a dispute with the miners which had forced the government to ration power and cut the working week to three days. In the midst of this late-winter gloom, the colleges were fighting to keep a loosely based association which would allow them to retain control over the design of courses and teaching of students. The Department on the other hand was still pressing for a much stronger central federal institute with appropriate powers. Hugh Harding astutely recognized the ultimate consequence for the colleges. In a letter dated 27 June 1974, he wrote that 'the institute could not be fully effective so long as the physical assets of the colleges of which it was composed were owned by different bodies. In the long term, we might hope that all property would be vested in the institute … but we recognize that it would be unrealistic to think that this stage could be reached for a good many years to come'.

The emergence of the institute owed much to the leadership of the independent chairman of the Formation Committee. Dr James Topping, the former Vice-Chancellor of Brunel University, took up the challenge in February 1974. He had overseen the transition of Brunel from technical college to university. As committee chairman he was, remembered Dorothy Bell, 'a wonderfully wise man', coaxing the four colleges to work more closely together. The three denominational colleges all received the backing of their providing bodies for the move towards the institute. The new Principal of Froebel, Michael Morgan, was fully supportive, demonstrating a more realistic appraisal of the situation than some staff and governors who were still hostile to the idea of a secular institution combining with three denominational colleges. This opposition became more muted as other colleges began closing, including all the local education authority colleges.

By now, Roy Knight was describing the imminent formation of the new organization with great excitement. The Formation Committee had spawned various other committees and groups. Publicity was given a high priority from the outset for the institute had little time to make itself known and attract students for the new courses when it was now competing with the polytechnics and others. A Joint Interim Academic Planning Body, in effect a shadow Senate, as the Formation Committee was a shadow Council, was established and oversaw the detailed work needed before the new institute could take effect in September 1975. Work on the new courses had begun even in advance of the creation of the Formation Committee. The BEd and Certificate of Education would continue, to which would be added the Diploma in Higher Education, combined BA and BSc honours degrees and an innovation, the Bachelor of Humanities degree. The latter, known as the BHum, was devised to overcome the objections of ULIE to awarding the BA for courses where one of the two subjects offered, such as movement studies, was not taught as an undergraduate course in any of the colleges. The courses were submitted to ULIE for scrutiny in early 1974 but approval was given only in the summer of 1975, even though they had featured in RIHE's marketing material the year before.

Several options for the name of the new institute were considered. Most of them were too long – the South West London Voluntary Colleges Association and the South West London Institute of Higher Education. As a new body, a shorter name was desirable if it was to have any impact on prospective students. When the title of Wandsworth Institute of Higher Education was discounted, it was finally agreed to call the new body the Roehampton Institute of Higher Education (RIHE). Roy Knight succinctly summed up how the participating colleges defined the new organization – RIHE would be 'a federation of the four colleges: the social, religious and community life of each college will continue independently on its own site, as will a great deal of the teaching; but in academic terms the total resource of the four will be available in planning the courses for any one of the 3,000 students'. In addition, with 1,800 places still reserved for trainee teachers, RIHE would be responsible for training a third of all teachers in London and more than any other institution in England.

James Topping skilfully persuaded the colleges and the DES to accept an organization which was a compromise for both of them. While the DES wanted RIHE to have total responsibility for all teaching, including the appointment of all staff, the Department finally agreed that every member of staff would be assigned to a specific college. The Department gave up the fight to abolish the posts of Principals and Vice-Principals, whom the colleges continued to appoint themselves, and also permitted the colleges to carry on admitting their own students. In the autumn of 1974 the colleges' governing bodies agreed to join RIHE. They did have a get-out clause, which entitled any college to withdraw from RIHE by giving five years' notice, either during 1980–2 or 1996–7.

At last, on 9 July 1975, the DES formally approved the creation of RIHE. This was the first federal scheme of reorganization in the country – other voluntary colleges had either amalgamated or been absorbed by other institutions. The Secretary of State noted in his approval letter that 'the successful negotiation of the agreement between the four colleges therefore represents a major new initiative in the field of higher and further education'. Two more would follow, Chelmer Institute of Higher Education, based on the former Brentwood College, and West London Institute of Higher Education, created from the Borough Road and Maria Grey colleges.

Nearly 900 students had been enrolled for September 1975. They were almost evenly divided between those studying for degrees and those taking the Certificate

Students in class, 1976.

Skylight detail, The Terrace, Grove House.

of Education, although, taking into account those opting for the BEd, most students were still training to become teachers. With students and staff moving throughout the day from one college to another, depending on what and where they were studying or teaching, the administrative arrangements for making the whole thing work were regarded as a triumph. The experience of Raywen Ford, who came to study at Froebel in 1978 as a married mother of two, was typical – she went to Southlands for art education, to Froebel for education studies, to Digby Stuart for practical art and to Whitelands for the history of art education. It is easy to forget that only two colleges at the time, Froebel and Digby Stuart, were next to each other; Southlands was still in Wimbledon and Whitelands in Putney. The inter-collegiate bus service and the interchangeable meal passes and library tickets only highlighted the inherent strain within the system. So too did the agreement of the colleges to transfer the control and maintenance of their assets to RIHE but only within clearly defined limits. It was, wrote Peter Weston, 'a foretaste of the complexity that would frustrate decision-making in the newly-formed Institute'.

RIHE saved the four colleges. At Froebel, for instance, overall numbers remained around 650 throughout the 1970s, when other colleges were closing or shrinking in size. This achievement disguised the fact that in 1977 the 55 places for trainee teachers at the College reflected a cut of 75 per cent compared with 1967. The difference was made up by students taking the new degree courses. Higher degrees were also instituted, the first, an MA in Education, being approved by ULIE in 1974 before RIHE was established. An MA in Music Education followed in 1975. Whitelands fared less well, with numbers falling from 900 to 600 by 1977, but the decline would have been even steeper without the ability to attract students for the new courses.

In 1976 RIHE appointed its first Rector. Dr Kevin Keohane came from Chelsea College where he had been Vice-Principal. Clear-sighted and visionary, he too, like Sister Mary Richardson, saw the germ of a university at Roehampton and encouraged academic ambition. His affability and vitality helped him to secure the continued cooperation of the four colleges. Previously a governor of Digby Stuart, he valued the colleges. In turn, the College Principals, who had become close friends through working together to create RIHE and save the colleges, were unstinting in their support of the Institute. Each of them in turn acted as Deputy Rector and they all met the Rector weekly. This mutually supportive relationship was symbolized in Senate and Council meeting in turn at each of the colleges. This makes Keohane's task sound easier than it was for those two bodies were dominated by representatives of the colleges. On Council in particular members tended to think in terms of what was in the best interests of their own college rather than of RIHE as a whole.

Creating some sort of unity within the Institute was complicated by the fact that at the same time the Rector had to eliminate the duplication of provision which had occurred when RIHE was formed. He also had to find places for new staff for he was acutely aware that

Above: Teacher training, 1976.

Opposite: Movement studies, 1976.

teaching at degree level was very different from teaching the same subjects for teacher training. RIHE was clearly overstaffed. In the year of Keohane's appointment, RIHE had 300 staff for 3,000 students. Over the next three years staff numbers were cut back by almost 20 per cent. Simultaneously, the Rector started to build up individual departments, appointing their heads through open advertisement, as RIHE began the slow process of admitting able external candidates as one way of raising the academic calibre of staff. It was understandable that this process was often resented by older, long-serving members of staff. In fact, Roy Knight had recognized the need for renewal among staff several years earlier when he had written of the need to sustain the reputation enjoyed by Whitelands by appointing 'lively new talents'. And open advertisement did give opportunities to existing staff – Peter Weston, for instance, who had joined Froebel in 1970 as an English lecturer, was appointed head of the English department in 1980. He would eventually retire as Deputy Vice-Chancellor of the independent university in 2005.

Although every encouragement was given to existing staff who wished to pursue higher degrees, there were definitely two camps among the staff at RIHE in the late 1970s. One consisted of those, usually among the older generation, intent on retaining the influence of the colleges and the other of those who even then saw RIHE developing as a quasi-university. Some older staff found they were regarded almost as second-class citizens because they were uninterested in research and were disconcerted by newly appointed staff who both taught and researched. Many new staff, appointed by RIHE rather than the colleges, were eager to see departments moving to one central location rather than being split among the colleges.

RIHE finally became a legal entity in December 1978. James Topping, who had chaired both RIHE's Council and Senate in the interim, finally stood down. In his place came Professor W.A. Campbell, a former Vice-Chancellor of Keele University. Topping's contribution had been immense and invaluable. So too had that of the various College Principals, who had seen early on that the colleges could survive only through cooperation. While many of those around them, including some of those on their governing bodies, found it difficult to look beyond their college walls, the Principals quickly accepted the fact that the future prosperity and reputation of the colleges was intertwined with that of the new organization. Ultimately, of course, they had a duty towards the colleges, but the mutual understanding which they developed with the Rector was instrumental in beginning that long process leading towards the eventual integration of their separate interests. The Rector would later be generous in his praise for their help – 'the formation and progress of the federal Institute would have been much more difficult without the contribution which has been made by the Principals of the four colleges. Their presence not only ensured the continuing commitment to a meaningful collegiate structure but enabled the transition from four unitary institutions to a single federal institute to proceed relatively smoothly'.

TOWARDS FEDERATION
1980–2000

The distant vision of an independent university at Roehampton came gradually closer during the last 20 years of the century, pursued with increasing vigour by successive rectors. An important part of this progress was a new relationship with the University of Surrey. So too was the appointment of new staff and the encouragement of existing staff to further their qualifications, helping to raise standards. RIHE began to develop distinctive strengths, including dance, linguistics and early childhood studies. There was progress too, however slow and haphazard, towards a more effective central administration, which went hand in hand with attempts to create a single campus at Roehampton. After 1997, the renewed expansion of higher education, which aimed for the participation of half of all 18-year-olds, gave a further boost to Roehampton's ambitions.

Above: Students in the Digby Stuart bar, 1982.

Opposite: Charities week, 1982.

In December 1979 the University of London announced that it would cease to validate courses for colleges linked with ULIE beyond those students taking up places in the autumn of 1983. Ostensibly, the decision was made because the University believed that ULIE was unsuited for the validation of courses which now covered many more subjects other than education. But, as the historian of ULIE wrote, 'within the University there was a widespread view that the associated colleges and their courses had become an encumbrance'. Some of the colleges concerned turned to the Council for National Academic Awards (CNAA), the body which regulated the polytechnics, for validation, and the DES expected RIHE to follow suit. But Kevin Keohane sought a new relationship with another university. Instead of tying RIHE to the CNAA, which might hinder RIHE's future academic ambitions, the Rector believed his strategy of broadening RIHE's outlook would be best helped by a partnership with another established university. The obvious partner was the University of Surrey, some 30 miles distant in Guildford. As a university with technological roots, it appeared to complement RIHE's own strengths. Surrey was receptive and RIHE's request for validation was approved on 29 January 1980. Validation visits were made throughout 1980 and 1981 and the first students on award programmes validated by Surrey entered RIHE in 1982. The first students with University of Surrey degrees graduated from RIHE at a ceremony in Guildford Cathedral in 1985.

The relationship generally worked well. As the validating authority, Surrey interfered little. Partly this was because RIHE's courses were thoroughly scrutinized

Above: Digby Stuart Students' Union on an outing, 1982.

Below: A child participating in a student project, 1982.

within the Institute to ensure that high standards were maintained and partly because the liberal arts and social sciences which dominated the courses offered by RIHE were almost entirely foreign to Surrey. Members of the English Department, for instance, were delighted that Surrey did not have its own department, for they had resented the bureaucratic procedures and sometimes supercilious attitude taken by ULIE validating examiners. On the other hand, the broad first-year course in history initially prescribed by Surrey was regarded by RIHE staff as ineffective, who labelled it disdainfully as 'Plato to Nato'. Attempts were made to foster closer cooperation between the two organizations but the disparity between the courses as well as the distance between them prevented much in the way of shared teaching.

As more staff joined RIHE from other academic institutions, so many existing staff achieved higher degrees. In 1983, for instance, four members of staff at Whitelands received doctorates. Among the new wave of staff joining RIHE in the early 1980s was John Seed. Attached to Southlands, he was mistaken for a student when he first entered the senior common room. The divide between those staff who had been stalwarts of the training colleges and those newly appointed academic staff intent on research as well as teaching was still obvious. But Seed found himself warmly welcomed and discovered that often there was little to distinguish between long-serving staff and their younger peers in terms of intellect. They simply regarded intellectual pursuits as a vocation, rather than a profession, and their lack of interest in research, as opposed to teaching, disguised the fact that they were often very well

Teaching practice, 1980s.

read. Bernadette Porter, who joined RIHE in 1983, discovered that staff were given every Thursday specifically to conduct research. A student at Digby Stuart in the early 1970s, she returned to teach in the education department, located in Froebel College. The Principal, Michael Morgan, insisted she should be addressed in a non-denominational college as 'Miss' rather than 'Sister'.

Although encouraging research was a high priority, there was always a consciousness that this should not be at the cost of the fine teaching reputation the colleges had established. Existing staff were given the opportunity to gain higher qualifications precisely because of their teaching skills, a quality always sought in new appointments. And the way in which

Left: Whitelands May Day celebrations, 1986.

Below: Whitelands, 1980s.

staff were appointed often reflected the traditions inherited from the colleges. Jennifer Coates took up her first permanent academic post at RIHE at the age of 41 in 1984. She appreciated the belief in her ability shown by those who appointed her at an age when she would have been discounted by other institutions. She found a vibrant department full of able men and women, often maverick, sometimes difficult, who were stimulating teachers, regardless of their academic backgrounds. She was also conscious that staff were pretty well balanced between men and women, making it noticeably different from the male-dominated departments in some other universities.

Having departments spread across the colleges was only ever going to be a short-term policy. As well as being inefficient, it hindered departmental development. Zachary Leader, who joined the English department in 1976, discovered it was divided into college factions, each with separate offices, even with separate reading lists. In the early 1980s John Seed had a distinct timetable for every one of the colleges in which he taught and found he rarely met his fellow historians. Even when Trevor Dean was appointed to lecture in Renaissance history in 1987, the history department still had offices in each college, involving a great deal of travelling. Concentrating each department in one location, a gradual process spread over several years, was a major step forward and entirely in keeping with the philosophy which had led to the creation of RIHE in the first place. The pressure for change originally came in 1982 when at least two departments were asking to be based in one college only. It was unpopular with some who saw it as yet another move towards centralization, further eroding the role of the colleges and, as far as the Principal of Southlands, Douglas Millbank, was concerned, even threatening their integrity. But the request was supported by Kevin Keohane, who saw it as an opportunity to extend the process to other departments. He made his argument for change in a gently persuasive way. He pointed out that it was impossible for RIHE, given the provision of diversified, multi-subject degrees, the appointment of specialist staff and limited facilities, to continue to offer discrete teaching within each college, and that teaching had to be conducted on a federal rather than a collegiate basis. The paper he presented to Council in February 1983 shrewdly made no reference to centralization in its title, 'Localiation of Departments'. It could only be a work in progress, for while drama was relocated to Digby Stuart, art to Froebel and languages to Whitelands, it was impossible for the time being to find the space to do the same for all departments, including English and history. The only department unaffected was education, too large to transfer to one site. Bringing departmental staff together in one place created a camaraderie previously lacking. It was a policy supported by most staff, especially those recently appointed without any strong attachment to the colleges. Some were impatient to see it extended, wanting to see a single campus with centralized resources. For many years, for example, there was neither a university library nor a unified library catalogue, with lecturers having to visit each college library to determine which books were available. It was only in the mid-1990s that funding for a central library was secured, when Digby Stuart generously provided an entire accommodation block for conversion.

The absence of a central library was partly because of the major reductions in spending suffered by the higher education sector during the 1980s. Since RIHE's federal structure made it more expensive to run than similar organizations, the impact of budget cuts after 1983 accelerated centralization. The corollary of rationalizing college administration, with reduced responsibilities for College Principals, was strengthening central administration. It also meant further job losses among

An art installation, PGCE, 1980.

staff which, coming so soon after the major redundancies initiated in the late 1970s, did little for morale. The cutbacks made at Whitelands were typical – in the early 1980s they included abandoning nursing, welfare, counselling and accommodation services, reducing by half the level of cleaning and maintenance and the early retirement of the Principal; a little later on, more cuts led to the loss of a dozen lecturing posts as well as ancillary workers, and further reductions in spending on cleaning and maintenance and student services.

Whether in planning the administrative development of the Institute or in striving to find financial economies, the Rector was always conscious of the need to maintain the support of the colleges. When departments were moved out of colleges, for instance, he made sure that new staff were still allocated to a specific college so that as wide a spread of academic interests as possible was represented. He knew that the backing of the College Principals was essential, particularly when the colleges still had the option to withdraw from the Institute. As compensation for the diminution of their college responsibilities as a consequence of budget cuts, and to maintain their standing within the Institute, all the Principals were appointed Pro-Rectors in 1983. The

Above: Pope John Paul II talking to Sister Dorothy Bell, during his visit to Digby Stuart in 1982.

impact of the cuts had aroused strong feelings among college governing bodies. At Southlands, governors complained that their influence in decision making had been largely neutered since the formation of RIHE. As a result of this, and with the aim of improving communications with the colleges, a collegiate committee was established in 1984, including representatives of governing and providing bodies.

In these early years of the Institute students tended to remain loyal to their own colleges. Partly this was because of the distance between them, partly because of differing traditions. The first intercollegiate RAG week eventually took place in 1980 and the Roehampton chorus and orchestra performed with their peers from the University of Surrey but otherwise there was little enthusiasm for intercollegiate activities or cooperation, even in sport. One major event which did bring staff and students together from across the Institute was the visit of Pope John Paul II on 29 May 1982. Sister Dorothy Bell had been asked to make the grounds of Digby Stuart College available for an early morning service attended by the Pope. It attracted more than 5,000 people. The changing character of the student population was reflected in the formation of an Asian Society with Hindu, Muslim, Sikh, Jewish and Christian

Above: HRH The Princess Royal smiling broadly on being introduced to the Whitelands May King, Jason Scanlon (inset), by Canon David Peacock on a visit to the College in 1991.

Below: Dance instruction, 1980s.

members. Another sign of the times was the election in 1986 of Whitelands student Gary Lynch as the first May King.

By the early 1980s there were some 2,600 students at the Institute. Of these, 2,100 were taking degrees, with nearly two-thirds studying non-education courses and almost 80 per cent achieving good honours degrees. Whitelands in 1983, for instance, had more than 600 students, comprising 385 women and 116 men on full-time courses, of whom 230 were resident and three-fifths were taking non-education degree courses. 'To have moved in barely two decades,' wrote the Rector, 'from two- or three-year Certificate courses to degrees in Education and 19 other disciplines and to have substantially increased the in-service programmes has been a major achievement, particularly when regard is paid to the resources available.'

Building on the record of the four colleges, education continued to be one of the Institute's great assets. In 1983, when the government expanded primary teacher training, RIHE was one of the four institutions invited to cater for this increase. Three years later, drawing on the expertise of Froebel College, the Centre for Early Childhood Studies was established in Grove House, focusing on early years teaching and in-service training for nursery education. This was followed in 1992 by the Centre for Development in Primary Education.

The Institute also capitalized on other strengths inherited from the colleges. Movement and dance owed much to Mollie Davies, who had joined Froebel in 1958, and became Head of Dance at the Institute. She had helped to create the degree programmes in movement studies and dance studies. She had co-directed and choreographed one of the first dance collectives to take contemporary dance into schools and colleges. In 2005 the new dedicated building for dance would be named after and opened by her. When she retired in 1992, her work was developed by her successor Professor Stephanie Jordan, who continued to expand the department.

As well as building on past foundations, the Institute welcomed innovation. Jennifer Coates and Deborah Cameron (later Rupert Murdoch Professor of Language and Communication at Oxford University) pioneered the new English language course, developing a reputation as the two leading feminist linguistics academics in the country. They developed an innovative course which became known as Language, Society and Power, demonstrating how sexism, racism, ageism and identity were all reflected in and implied by language.

STEPHEN HOLT

Stephen Campbell Holt was born in 1935 and educated at Mill Hill School and Emmanuel College, Cambridge. He completed his MA in 1963 and his doctorate in 1966 and became a respected academic in the field of political science. After lecturing at Sheffield University, he was appointed Professor of European Studies at Bradford in 1970 and moved to the University of Kent to take up the same post in 1980. At both universities he held the position of Pro Vice-Chancellor. He was appointed to Roehampton as Rector in 1988, playing an invaluable part in developing the academic and organizational strength of the organization as part of his ultimate objective for the Institute to achieve independent university status. A man of liberal and humane views, as well as a convinced internationalist, he retired in 1999 after sealing the agreement to create the federal University of Surrey. He died in 2001.

The first Readers were appointed by the Institute in 1988. This was not only an acknowledgement of the quality of the academics at the Institute who regarded themselves as both teachers and researchers but also another step on the way in the Institute's own academic development. Two years previously, four faculties had been created, with Martin Shipman confirmed in his post as Dean of Education, Peter Weston named as Dean of Humanities, Gordon Brand as Dean of Social Studies and Felix Fifer as Dean of Sciences. The Rector still maintained his vision of the Institute as an independent university, telling Weston that, as far as he was concerned, 'there is no future in any other direction'. The Institute had already investigated the possibility of becoming University College, Roehampton, and applying for polytechnic status, but both of these had come to nothing.

Kevin Keohane retired in 1988. His successor was Professor Stephen Holt, a political scientist and Pro Vice-Chancellor at the University of Kent. A likeable, principled man, sympathetic to the liberal arts culture of the Institute, he shared the organization's

Opposite: Grove House portico.

Right: Language lab, Whitelands, 1980s.

aspirations for higher academic status. His appointment from a shortlist which included several candidates from the polytechnics was a clear indication of the path the Institute wished to take.

During his first year in office Holt was persuaded by Gillian Redford, the recently appointed Principal of Froebel, that the Institute should seek accreditation by Surrey. As well as certifying the quality of the courses offered by RIHE, accreditation would also give the Institute greater responsibility for its own academic decisions. It seemed a logical next step towards the Institute's ultimate goal. In 1991 RIHE became the first organization to receive accreditation from its validating university. It was a considerable accomplishment for an Institute less than 20 years old.

In the same year Holt persuaded Senate to introduce modular courses. This was an integral part of Holt's personal vision for RIHE. He believed that for the Institute to flourish in a higher education sector which was becoming increasingly competitive, it needed to attract a new generation of potential students who had never before considered higher education. Modular courses, allowing multi-subject degrees, were attractive to part-time students, who could study one module at a time, gaining credits towards full honours degree. There were drawbacks – such courses were criticized for disrupting the developmental approach to learning while funding policies requiring students to graduate within a stipulated timescale undermined the concept of students interrupting completion of their modules by taking time out to pursue a career. Modular courses brought one other change, with the introduction of semesters in 1993 to reduce the frequency of assessments and visits by external examiners.

By then RIHE had achieved another landmark. In 1992 the government decided to reclassify all polytechnics as universities. This decision left RIHE, with its singular status and distinct identity, feeling isolated, but all colleges of higher education still had the option of seeking degree-awarding powers. The feeling among most staff that RIHE's standards made it worthy of awarding its own degrees was a sign of the Institute's growing confidence. Under Peter Weston, recently appointed Assistant Rector, a huge amount of time and effort was invested in the application. It was backed by remarkably good results from the Institute's participation in the first Research Assessment Exercise (RAE) in 1992, which demonstrated the fruits of the academic appointments and further qualifications gained by existing staff during the late 1970s and throughout the 1980s. The application was approved in 1993 but only for the power to award taught rather than research degrees. The government had changed the rules in the meantime and RIHE was told that it must delay for five years any application

Physics class, 1980s.

Above: Two students in a Southlands bedroom, 1980s.

Above right: Scenes from the Southlands Library.

for the power to award research degrees. This was disappointing for Stephen Holt and many others who wanted RIHE to achieve university status as soon as possible. Changed circumstances made it impossible for this to occur much earlier than 2000. On the other hand, following RIHE's showing in the first RAE, the Institute would have more time to develop its research activities. For Stephen Holt, RIHE's success in this sphere, gaining increasing sums for research from responsible government organization, was invaluable so that, as he wrote, 'for the foreseeable future we can avoid being sucked into the whirlpool of becoming a "teaching only" university'. The nature of the organization was changing fundamentally.

Stephen Holt was developing another idea intended to strengthen the Institute prior to any application for university status. Believing that RIHE benefited from offering the degrees of an established and respected university, which gave some protection from its major London rivals, he was reluctant for the Institute to award its own taught degrees while it was still validated by Surrey. Instead, he wanted to forge an even stronger relationship. After a visit to the University of Manchester and the University of Manchester Institute of Technology in 1992, he was enthusiastic to create a similar single academic community albeit with each body controlling their own finances, assets, staff and students. The notion did not appeal to the then Vice-Chancellor of Surrey, Professor Anthony Kelly, but his successor, Professor Patrick Dowling, appointed in 1995, was more enthusiastic. Dowling believed this would favour Surrey as much as RIHE, even leading to a wider federation embracing several other universities and colleges, an ambition ultimately never met. While Dowling accepted that RIHE would eventually wish to pursue independent university status, he and Holt agreed that in the interim RIHE might be best served by developing a federal relationship with Surrey. This qualification was made explicit in the protocol signed in June 1995 which agreed that RIHE should be designated as an Institute of the University of Surrey – 'The University recognizes that the Institute may at some time in the future wish to become an independent university and award its own degrees.' RIHE agreed to give two years' notice of any such intention. In fact, federation was still

The Quad at Southlands, Wimbledon, 1980s.

more than four years away; discussions would not be concluded until after RIHE had received the power to award research degrees.

In the meantime RIHE's academic growth continued. Education remained central to the Institute. Under Tina Bruce and others, the Froebelian philosophy of education became more rigorous, and won more converts nationally. Early Childhood Studies, in addition to becoming a degree programme in its own right in the late 1990s, became more wide ranging, recognizing the need for a broader qualification for professionals involved with young children outside teaching, initiating a trend which would be widely emulated at other institutions. RIHE, for instance, was among the first bodies to offer a postgraduate diploma in Early Childhood Studies, which attracted social workers and health workers as well as teachers. During the 1990s this new-found confidence was also exemplified by the revival of the award of Froebel Certificates after a gap of more than 30 years.

Stephen Holt backed staff in the English department who wished to begin a degree course in Women's Studies. Out of a series of rather haphazardly organized meetings came a course which in a year had been validated and was being taught to the first small group of students. For Jennifer Coates and others, it was tremendously exciting to be involved in starting something which set the trend. Part of the social science faculty, rather than the arts and humanities faculty, the course made all sorts of cross-curricular connections, covering, for instance, the gender of geography as well as women writers and feminist theology. Although the course is no longer taught, it gave rise to many gender-linked courses within the university curriculum. Another departure was a course which eventually became a full single honours degree in linguistics and led to the creation of a separate department. Giving staff the freedom to devise their own specialist courses was becoming one of RIHE's strengths. Among the first professors appointed by RIHE were Zachary Leader and Jennifer Coates, who was one of several women to be appointed.

Stephen Holt's emphasis on RIHE's academic growth led some of the colleges and their providing bodies to feel neglected. Soon after Holt's appointment, the colleges had felt aggrieved at a further blow to their independence when budgets were centralized, although there were those, including at least one Principal, who were surprised that the colleges had been able to retain so much financial independence for so long. In the case of Southlands, this tension had led the Methodist Conference to refuse to adopt the College's annual report in 1991.

Right: Inspecting skulls in a laboratory, Southlands, 1980s.

Below: Student play, Southlands, 1980s.

The Rector was also suspected of wishing to secularize the Institute on the way to university status. This was probably unfair. Stephen Holt was a religious man whose unorthodox views made him sympathetic not only to the ethos of every one of the colleges but to those of non-Christian faiths. It was with his encouragement that RIHE formed the Jewish Resource Centre in 1996 as a joint project with the local Jewish community. As RIHE's student population altered, with an increasing number from other faiths, Holt also talked about creating a fifth faith-based college, this time for Muslims. Buildings were identified and potential sponsors were approached but a lack of enthusiasm from some staff and within the colleges led the project to peter out.

Recognizing the need to improve relations with the colleges, Stephen Holt revived Kevin Keohane's practice of appointing College Principals as Pro-Rectors in 1992. Bernadette Porter, who had succeeded Dorothy Bell as Principal of Digby Stuart in

1987, became Pro-Rector with responsibility for finance and staffing. She believed that these appointments created a much better mutual understanding among senior management as well as a strong personal bond. She also felt that this helped the Principals to appreciate that RIHE as a whole was greater than the sum of its parts, encouraging them to work with their own governing and providing bodies towards greater cooperation with the Institute.

In truth, this was already happening, for the colleges, as founders of RIHE, had always had a vested interest in the organization's growing success. Whatever reservations they may have shared about the path taken by RIHE, however much they may have kicked over the traces, the colleges shared with Holt and his predecessor the vision of a single, united academic institution. In 1992, for instance, the colleges agreed to transfer to Council most of the business conducted by the collegiate committee. Even more radically, the providing bodies had also expressed a willingness to consolidate into a single trust the property they owned and leased to RIHE, although turning this into a reality would prove to be much more long-term. While Keohane had concentrated on the Institute's academic organization, Holt focused on the development of a single campus. When the issue was raised with the colleges in 1988, it was suggested that either Southlands and Whitelands would relocate to sites in Roehampton or the Institute would move to a completely new campus, possibly near Guildford. The latter was quickly discounted as impractical. There were

Above: Artist's impression of Southlands College at Roehampton.

Below: The 'Mother and Child' sculpture by Ernst Eisenmayer was moved to the College's new site in Roehampton.

Right: Laying the foundation stone for Southlands College, 1996.

LESLIE GRIFFITHS, BARON GRIFFITHS OF BURRY PORT

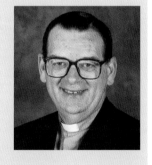

Born in 1942, Leslie Griffiths was educated at Llanelli Grammar School and graduated from Cambridge in 1969. Becoming a local preacher with the Methodist Church in 1963, his extensive work for Methodism saw him serve overseas as well as in the UK. He was President of the Methodist Conference in 1994–5. In 1996 he became Superintendent Minister of Wesley's Chapel in London. He has written and broadcast extensively. He was involved with Southlands College for many years, latterly as chairman of the college governing body, and sat as a member of the Council at Roehampton until 2003. He gave the sermon at the service of inauguration for the University of Surrey at Roehampton at Westminster Abbey in 2000.

clear advantages in striving towards a single campus – it would make possible a central library, save money by rationalizing administration and cutting the cost of bussing students between colleges, and improve the quality of life for students and staff. In addition, the buildings then occupied by Whitelands and Southlands were ageing and obsolescent, beyond the means of either college to adapt for modern purposes, even had that been a practical proposition.

The governing body of Southlands took a long time to agree that the College should move to Roehampton. The governors had many reservations and had even discussed whether or not the College should remain in RIHE. When they finally made up their minds in in 1991, the decision did not go down well with some members of the Southlands Society, frightened the College would lose its identity. In fact, this was just one more move for the College which, like the other three, had never shrunk from moving to more appropriate premises in the past when it was obviously in its best interests. In February 1994 it was agreed to build a new college on a site acquired from Digby Stuart, which once again displayed a generosity of spirit in the interest of the Institute as a whole. The site was popularly known as 'the South of France' from the time when schoolgirls had used the area for picnics on sunny summer days. The newly formed Southlands Trustees oversaw the sale of the Wimbledon property and the transfer of the College to Roehampton. Southlands at Roehampton would open free from debt, with a surplus from which the College would make a contribution towards the new central library and learning resource centre. The foundation stone was laid in June 1996 and the College was formally

opened in October 1997 by the Vice-President of the Methodist Conference, the former Director-General of the BBC, Sir Michael Checkland. The names of the new buildings, arranged around a fountain quadrangle, reflected the College's Methodist heritage – Wesley Hall, Aldersgate Court and Epworth Court. The Queen kindly gave her consent for the main teaching block to be called the Queen's Building.

Whitelands too debated the idea of relocation, but was as sensitive as Southlands to the possible loss of college identity. The College magazine noted in 1989 that 'the College dimension … must be preserved at all costs and any move by Whitelands from its present accommodation would need to be accompanied by cast-iron assurances that the College's Anglican foundation, ethos, traditions and right to a considerable measure of self-government would continue to be respected'.

At the same time, the governing body had to take into account the escalating cost of outstanding maintenance on the ageing existing buildings, estimated to be £12 million, of which the state would contribute just ten per cent. The buildings were also under pressure from overcrowding. In the summer of 1990 a feasibility report concluded that a move to a site in Roehampton would be to the academic, social and financial advantage of the College, and the Principal, David Peacock, was convinced that relocation was a necessity. But the furore the idea aroused among some staff and former students proved much stronger than at Southlands. They pressed for and succeeded in having the existing buildings listed in the belief this would make the site unattractive

Top left: The Southlands College bicycle, used by students for running errands in Wimbledon before World War Two, now on display at Roehampton.

Top right: Stained glass in the Southlands Chapel.

Above: May King Kojo Kyereme in 1997. He went on to marry his attendant, Fiona Cole, who is behind him in the photograph.

to developers and prevent any relocation taking place. The controversy, combined with some doubt whether the prospective site at Froebel would be large enough for new buildings sufficiently large to cater for an expanding student body, put paid to any early decision. But sooner or later the College would have to move because the existing accommodation was no longer suitable and no amount of money spent on it would remedy the situation. Plans for improvements and additions were made, including a group of five new halls, which were the least that could be done, commented the College magazine in 1992, if Whitelands at Putney was not to become just 'an unloved, and perhaps ultimately unwanted, annexe of the Roehampton Institute'. Five years later, however, even as these plans were being implemented, David Peacock felt a rising surge of anger as he attended the opening of Southlands in Roehampton that similar opportunities had been denied Whitelands. He was encouraged to raise the topic once more, and helped by the lack of any real opposition, given the obvious advantages

The Queen's Building in the snow.

enjoyed by Southlands, a decision had been made in principle for a move to take place by the time Peacock retired in 2000.

By then the government was encouraging a much higher proportion of young people to take up university places after leaving school. The composition of RIHE's student body was already much altered. In July 1997 the Whitelands College magazine remarked how the College's first black May King, Kojo Kyereme, was 'a living symbol of the College's increasingly multi-cultural and multi-ethnic make-up'. Many students were already coming from backgrounds where they were the first in their families to have entered university. The debate about funding student places was already taking place, the value of student grants had been steadily diminishing, and tuition fees were imminent, leaving many students from poorer backgrounds making up the gap by taking up part-time jobs during term-time, let alone during vacations. Another consequence was an upsurge in applications to RIHE from many potential students living close by, deterred financially from seeking places at institutions further from home. Often such students found the help they received from staff invaluable. One young man who came to Whitelands later looked back with gratitude at the ethos of welfare and respect at the College which had supported him with kindness as he struggled to mature: 'While it is tempting to exaggerate the effect that had on me, I think it would be hard to do so. I was hard work and I had a lot of growing up to do. The College made a conscious choice to support and help me.'

Below left: The Quad Conservatory, Southlands.

Below: Mike Leigh, Dr Bernadette Porter, Dr Trish Roberts, Dr Myszka Guzkowzka and Dr Peter Weston at May Day celebrations, 2001.

The Quad at Southlands, Roehampton.

College identity remained distinct but was inevitably diminished by the growth in the number of students at RIHE, most of whom were no longer resident. Whitelands was typical, changing from a community of around 600 students in the mid-1980s, most of whom were training to be teachers, to a more dispersed body of some 2,000 students by 2000, with trainee teachers in a minority and with many more part-time, mature and ethnic-minority students. Students now viewed the colleges as an integral part of the whole organization. This had led to the decision in the early 1990s, agreed by the student bodies in all the colleges, that the time had come to create a single students' union with one president, each college electing a deputy president.

In 1998 RIHE at last gained the right to award its own research degrees. It was well deserved. The sound results achieved in the 1992 RAE had been re-affirmed in the 1996 RAE, with drama, dance and the performing arts and theology, divinity and religious studies leading the way, closely followed by sports science, English language and literature, French and history. Winning research degree-awarding powers helped to conclude the negotiations over a federal partnership with the University of Surrey. Stephen Holt, who had worked so hard to raise the academic status of RIHE and whose brainchild the federation had been, retired in 1999, so it was his successor, Bernadette Porter, the Principal of Digby Stuart, who celebrated the creation of the University of Surrey Roehampton (USR) on 1 January 2000. By then, however, it seemed to many observers that the arrangement could only be short lived.

FROM FEDERATION TO INDEPENDENCE
2000–2004

Roehampton entered into the federation with Surrey in good faith but it quickly became clear that the organization had matured so rapidly during the 1990s and continued to do so in the early 2000s that this structure no longer had as much to offer. The spirited growth of the organization reflected the energetic leadership of Roehampton's new Rector. The consolidation of Roehampton's traditional teaching role was accompanied by the strengthening of its reputation for research. The fertile academic environment which had seen the development of linguistics, the expansion of dance and the introduction of Early Childhood Studies brought new developments, including children's literature, psychology, human rights and social justice. Further progress towards a more united campus came with the decision of Whitelands to move to another site half a mile away from the other three colleges. It was an action-packed few years, crowned by the achievement of independent university title in 2004.

Above: The National Centre for Research in Children's Literature (NCRCL) runs a flourishing postgraduate programme in children's literature.

Opposite: Whitelands today occupies a 14-acre site overlooking Richmond Park. At the heart of the College sits th e grade I listed Georgian villa, Parkstead House, which was built in the early 1760s. The house has been superbly renovated with stunning new architecture and buildings added to provide state-of-the-art facilities for students.

Previous spread: Graduation day, 2009.

The federal agreement was not a partnership of equals. Surrey, understandably, regarded itself as the senior partner, even though each institution had much the same number of students as well as a similar grant allocation from the government. The partnership had been pursued by Roehampton in the belief that association with an established university would strengthen its own development. The reality proved to be rather different. The enhanced profile Roehampton had believed would follow from the agreement did not materialize. While RIHE became University of Surrey Roehampton, Surrey did not, as had been expected, become University of Surrey Guildford, reinforcing the image of Roehampton as a junior partner. Surrey had also opposed the suggestion that Roehampton would benefit more from being called Roehampton University of Surrey rather than University of Surrey Roehampton. Whereas Roehampton had a distinct identity under its previous title, the new name caused confusion, which in the short term led to a fall in admissions to Roehampton. One member of staff was often asked if he still was at the same institution, so confused were some of his contacts by Roehampton's name changes.

Dr Suzy Jagger working with a computing student in the School of Business and Social Sciences.

94

There were a number of collaborative ventures, including the Centre for Research on Nationalism, Ethnicity and Multiculturalism (CRONEM), under the direction of John Eade, Professor of Sociology and Anthropology; the Centre for Applied and Professional Ethics; a taught MA in sociology; and the relocation of counselling and psychotherapy staff from Guildford to Roehampton. The Federal Innovations Fund also, for instance, allowed Robin Headlam-Wells, Professor of English Literature at Roehampton, to organize a pioneering symposium in May 2004. Entitled 'Literature, Science and Human Nature', and held at the ICA in London, it attracted major contributors, including Philip Pullman, Ian McEwan, Stephen Pinker and Joseph Carroll, and was a huge success. Federation also gave both partners the chance to learn from each other, which, in Roehampton's case, enhanced areas such as curriculum development and governance. But collaboration was not as extensive as had been hoped for and Surrey even began to compete in some of Roehampton's key areas, including English literature and dance and drama. The scope for academic synergy was also limited by the fact that Surrey had not adopted the system of modular courses practised at Roehampton. Given the dilution of Roehampton's identity, competition from Surrey in certain subjects and existing logistical disadvantages, federation arguably did less for Roehampton than its previous relationship with Surrey. It certainly did little to create any great sense of community between the two partners, even though the graduation ceremony for Roehampton students was held in Guildford Cathedral.

Roehampton's own development was increasing the confidence of staff that the organization was ready to become an independent university in its own right. This was certainly the view held by Roehampton's new Rector, Bernadette Porter, known to everyone as Bernie. Personally she had been surprised at her appointment but recognized that it was made because Roehampton needed someone with an existing depth of knowledge and understanding about the organization as it passed through a period of transition.

Clear and decisive about Roehampton's direction, she enjoyed the trust of her peers. Strengthening senior management by involving those responsible for both academic and non-academic aspects of Roehampton, she incidentally helped to create a senior team which included more women than for many years. Combined with a much higher proportion of female students, this helped to sustain the civilized and humane ethos derived in part from the traditions of

Above: Roehampton University's Archives and Special Collections Centre includes the Froebel Archive for Childhood Studies, the Children's Literature Collection and the Richmal Crompton Collection. The above illustration of William and his dog, Jumble, comes from Crompton's *Just William* series.

Below: Science student working in one of the new laboratories at Whitelands. The University's School of Human and Life Sciences is equipped with excellent laboratory facilities.

the four colleges and on which many new staff commented so favourably. The faculties and departments were replaced by eight schools in 2002, with the intention of creating a more responsive management structure. The blending of internal and external expertise continued, with four of the new heads of school appointed from outside Roehampton.

With her experience as a student at Digby Stuart, as well as her time as a College Principal, Bernie Porter was very conscious of the role of the colleges. They remained influential because of their representatives on Council, an influence which struck another Council member, Pauline Perry, who had played such a crucial part in the initiation of RIHE in 1975. Now Baroness Perry, she was appointed Chair of the Council at Roehampton in 2001. Bernie Porter was happy that the College Principals should continue to act as Pro-Rectors. With everyone working together to achieve independent university status, she felt that the colleges could be bound together more strongly in support of the wider organization, ameliorating the tension between the colleges and the centre which still surfaced from time to time. The colleges, she believed, were a great asset in defining the difference between Roehampton and other similar bodies. A survey revealed that the colleges remained important among students, who identified more strongly with their colleges the longer they remained at Roehampton.

Highlighting Roehampton's strengths, such as the colleges, was critical in marketing the organization when so many more students were entering higher education. The initial drop in applications following Roehampton's change of name emphasized the importance in making the organization more widely known, which it was hoped would also lessen Roehampton's dependence on clearing for filling places. This was a central aim of the 2001 strategic plan. Too many students were making Roehampton their second choice, encouraged by offers which were unnecessarily low. Partly this would be overcome as the confidence of staff increased, and partly by raising Roehampton's profile locally and nationally.

Roehampton University is a truly international organization welcoming students from over 130 countries. Students appreciate the supportive and stimulating learning environment and the proximity to central London.

PAULINE PERRY, BARONESS PERRY OF SOUTHWARK

Educated at Wolverhampton Girls' School and Girton College, Cambridge, Pauline Perry joined Her Majesty's Inspectorate at the Department of Education and Science in 1970. She became Chief Inspector of Schools in 1981. In 1986 she became Vice-Chancellor of South Bank Polytechnic, and with its transition to university status in 1992, was the first woman in the UK to take charge of a university. In 1994 she was appointed President of Lucy Cavendish College, Cambridge. Her extensive experience in higher education made her an ideal appointment in 2001 to chair the Council at Roehampton and she played a key role in guiding the Institute to full university status. She became an Honorary Fellow of the University in 2005.

Erasmus Mundus Human Rights MA students.

Engaging, charming and confident, Bernie Porter herself was an outstanding ambassador for Roehampton, becoming well known in higher education circles and sitting on the Schwartz committee on university admissions.

Applications to Roehampton soon began to rise once more. While dependency on clearing began to fall, in 2001 Roehampton made it easier for those seeking places through clearing by becoming the first London university to offer a clearing hotline via text messaging. The number of overseas students also increased, leading to the opening of an International Centre in 2001. By then, Roehampton had 350 international students, mainly from China, Japan and Norway.

There was plenty to attract potential students for Roehampton was a rising star. In the 2001 RAE music and dance was awarded the top 5* grading for international excellence in research. Research in anthropology and history, each with a grade 5, also attained international standards, while English language and literature and theology and religious studies received grade 4 for national excellence. At the same time Roehampton was already bringing a more professional approach to the management of research as it became an accepted part of the academic culture. In the School of Arts, for instance, the Research Committee scrutinized every application

submitted by staff, helped to formulate research programmes and introduced mentors to guide students in planning their research. The committee's scope also embraced the formation of international partnerships and conferences, establishing new research centres and offering workshops and seminars. At the same time there was a conscious decision to maintain a proper balance between research and teaching, for which Roehampton had a longstanding reputation.

Roehampton's achievements in the RAE attracted greater research funding. New research centres included those for International Research in Music Education, Research in Religious Education and Research in Human Rights. There were several joint ventures, including the Research Centre for Cross-Cultural Music and Dance Performance with Surrey and the School of African and Oriental Studies. The Centre for Hearth Tax Studies was established with backing from the Heritage Lottery Fund. Led by Emeritus Professor Margaret Spufford, the Centre was creating a database of all hearth tax records, publishing them in a regular series. Roehampton also hosted the National Centre for Research in Children's Literature, directed from 2004 by Dr Gillian Lathey.

Bernie Porter was keen to foster Roehampton's involvement in human rights and social justice. One of the many distinctive parts of Roehampton's make-up, this also drew on the tradition of the colleges, with their religious and philosophical foundation. In 2003, for instance, a special conference on human rights was held at Roehampton,

Students at Whitelands. The corridors are decorated with archival photographs and artefacts dating back to the College's foundation. The superb stained glass windows designed by Edward Burne-Jones in the late 19th century are displayed in the Victorian corridor at the heart of the College.

opened by the South African High Commissioner. Dance too was a distinctive thread, attracting more than 250 undergraduate students to study a wide range of dance-related topics. Roehampton's drama department, in which Maggie Pittard played an instrumental role until her retirement in 2002, was among the largest and most successful of any UK university. The School of Education Studies, formed from the former faculty of education, offered an extensive series of further degrees as well as in-service training and other courses. Roehampton's sports science degree, one of the longest established in the country, was also popular.

Many members of Roehampton's staff were gaining national and international recognition. Among them, Professor Stephanie Jordan and Dr Geraldine Morris produced in collaboration with the Royal Opera House a DVD featuring the dance and music styles of Sir Frederick Ashton in Stravinsky ballets as part of the celebrations for his centenary in 2004. Kevin Bales, Professor of Sociology, was a world expert on and fought for the abolition of contemporary slavery. Mike Watts, Professor of Science Education, was awarded a National Teaching Fellowship in 2003. Professor Peter Reynolds, Head of the School of Art, designed a performance-focused website for the National Theatre, which would win two BAFTA awards in 2005.

With Roehampton taking more relatively local students, there was greater involvement with the local community. This ranged from welcoming groups of gifted schoolchildren considering whether or not to embark on A levels to a project devised by English lecturers Dr Sarah Turvey and Professor Jenny Hartley to develop literary skills for offenders in the local prison at Wandsworth.

The relocation of Whitelands College to Roehampton moved a step nearer. The College governors were convinced of the need for new premises and planned initially to relocate the College to a site at the Roehampton Lane campus. But concerns

Below: In a recent Research Assessment Exercise (RAE) 100 per cent of Roehampton University's submitted work in Dance was recognized internationally or nationally for its originality, significance and rigour, with 55 per cent of that work regarded as being 'world-leading'.

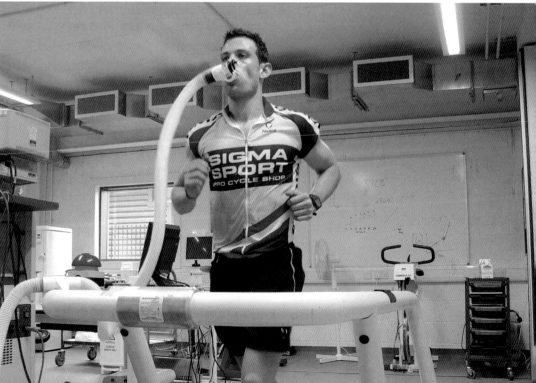

Right: Robyn Bond, studying for a degree in Sport and Exercise Sciences: 'A defining aspect of the programme is the access we are given to the most up-to-date equipment in the physiology and biomechanics labs.'

PARKSTEAD HOUSE

This beautiful neoclassical Palladian villa, located in the heart of Roehampton, was built by the eminent architect William Chambers for the second Earl of Bessborough in about 1762. The activities of Harriet, the wife of the third earl, a political hostess with a penchant for gambling and sex, gave colour to the early history of the house. She had two illegitimate children with another aristocrat, the Earl of Granville, while her legitimate daughter, who became Lady Caroline Lamb, had a similar reputation, most notoriously for her affair with Byron. In 1821, following Harriet's death, the house was leased to a banker, Abraham Robarts. It was sold on his death by the fifth earl in 1858 but subsequently resold in 1861 to the Society of Jesus. Renamed Manresa House after the town in Spain associated with Ignatius Loyola, the Society's founder, the Jesuits remained in occupation until 1962. Significant alterations and additions were made, including a new chapel. The poet Gerard Manley Hopkins was a novice here from 1868 to 1870, returning to teach for a year in 1873 and spending a further year in residence in 1881. With the encroachment of urban development, the Jesuits sold the property to London County Council and it became part of the Battersea College of Domestic Science in 1966. It was acquired as the new home of Whitelands College in 2001.

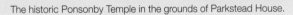

The historic Ponsonby Temple in the grounds of Parkstead House.

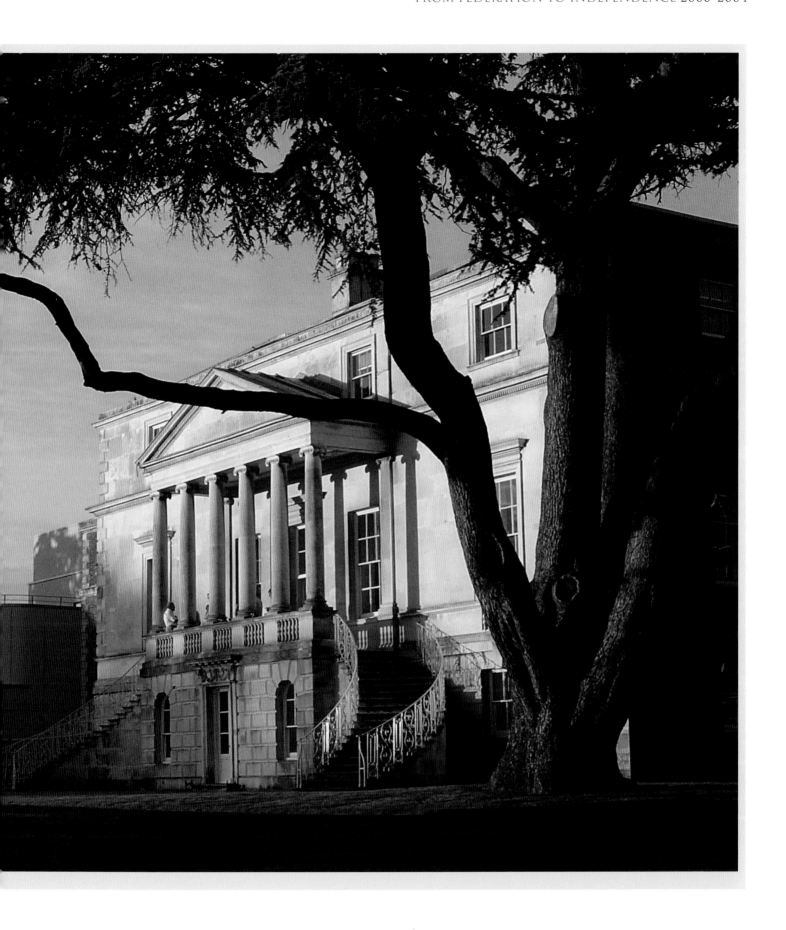

about the size of the site and any interest the College's providing body, the Church of England, might have, prompted the governors to search for an alternative. In December 2001 the College acquired the impressive Parkstead House, a grade 1 listed Georgian mansion in 14 acres of grounds, once a Jesuit seminary and associated with the poet Gerard Manley Hopkins, which lay just half a mile from the other colleges. The sale of the former college buildings for conversion into luxury apartments was concluded without controversy at the end of 2002 and in the spring of 2003 the College Principal, Dr Trish Roberts, announced a £30 million refurbishment and redevelopment programme, including a new chapel.

Above: The Chapel at Whitelands.

Above left: Detail of plasterwork at Parkstead House, Whitelands.

Below left: Students in the courtyard at Whitelands.

Opposite: Bernadette Porter, Roehampton's first Vice-Chancellor.

Working closely together, Bernie Porter and Pauline Perry both shared doubts about the long-term viability of the federation. They were concerned that Surrey was ambitious to extend the federation to embrace other similar institutions. This, they feared, would leave Roehampton in an even less influential position. Returning in 2003 from one meeting where the direction of the discussion seemed to confirm their anxieties, Pauline Perry asked Bernie Porter whether the time had not now arrived when Roehampton should apply to become an independent university. What made the timing propitious was a recent government invitation for non-university higher-education organizations to do just that. When the idea was put to Roehampton's Council in the autumn of 2003, it received warm support, as indeed it did from all the College Principals. At the same time Bernie Porter cleared the way for a successor to take Roehampton further forward by announcing that she would step down on completion of her term of office at the end of August 2004.

There was one hiccough. When College representatives heard that a successful application would have implications for the structure of Council, namely, that it would be much smaller and comprised of a majority of independent members, their enthusiasm waned somewhat. If Roehampton's bid was to succeed, it was important that the colleges gave their wholehearted support. Pauline Perry persuaded the Department for Education and Skills to consider a revised scheme. The Department, eager for Roehampton's bid to succeed, placed the proposal before the minister who was quick to agree.

Roehampton's decision was a disappointment to Surrey's Vice-Chancellor, but the Chairman of Surrey's Council, Sir William Wells, understood perfectly why it had been taken. In any case, it had been made clear when discussions about federation were first started in the mid-1990s that it would only ever be a short-term expedient. The decision was supported by almost every member of staff who saw it as a logical progression for Roehampton.

On 1 August 2004 Roehampton was awarded university title. Roehampton University was born. Fittingly, Bernie Porter became the new university's first Vice-Chancellor, although it was a title she held only briefly before she stepped down at the end of the month. Her contribution was nationally recognized with the award of the CBE in 2005.

ROEHAMPTON UNIVERSITY
2004 ONWARDS

Roehampton's independence gave its newly arrived Vice-Chancellor the chance to develop a clear identity for the University unhindered by the historical baggage of previous associations. But the values of the new University would draw heavily upon the traditions inherited from the four colleges and upon the distinctive academic characteristics steadily built up under RIHE. Most of the pieces of the jigsaw were already on the table; the first challenge for the Vice-Chancellor and his team was to put them together and create the unified organization Roehampton's new status demanded. Only as this crucial work was completed would it be possible to chart a longer-term course for the University.

Above: Professor Paul O'Prey became Vice-Chancellor of Roehampton University in 2004.

Opposite: Roehampton University has nearly 9,000 students. Accommodation, computer labs, sports facilities, a students' union, restaurants, drama workshops, TV studios, biomedical labs, teaching rooms and a learning resources centre are all located on the campus, allowing students direct access to the services and academic support vital to the successful completion of their studies.

Bernie Porter's successor was, like Stephen Holt, from an established university. Since 2002 Professor Paul O'Prey had been Director of Academic Affairs at Bristol University where he was also the long-serving Warden of Goldney Hall. Among other things at Bristol he had led the establishment of the University's enterprise and entrepreneurship programme. His first love had been English literature and after studying at Keble College, Oxford, he had spent time living with and working for the poet Robert Graves at his home in Mallorca. His research pursuits and publications, together with his leading role in the development of academic strategy in research and education at Bristol, met the criteria specified by his predecessor, who had urged Council to seek a serious intellectual who would turn a good teaching university into one of the best modern research universities. Like many Roehampton students, he had been the first member of his family to attend university. He quickly appreciated Roehampton's diversity, which he saw as one of its key strengths. Excited by the opportunities which lay ahead, he was eager for the University to become 'more entrepreneurial and outward looking'.

The University, he felt, needed to establish a strong and distinctive identity. He had been struck on his arrival by discovering that Roehampton's values were strongly held but not very clearly expressed or acted upon. One of his first tasks was to ask all those with any interest in the University for their views on what exactly Roehampton

Panoramic view of Digby Stuart.

A *Times Higher Education* survey ranked Roehampton 'first among London universities for the environment on and around campus'.

stood for. When that exercise concluded in December 2004, it summed up the University's purpose: challenging and supporting students in their intellectual and spiritual growth; preparing them to become citizens and leaders of a complex and fast-changing world; serving the communities on the University's doorstep; working for social justice; emphasizing the value of learning and the arts for nurturing the human spirit; engaging in the pursuit of truth through freedom of thought and expression; and promoting diversity, equality and tolerance.

This in turn led to a five-year plan launched in 2006, based on extending the University's reputation for high-quality teaching and research, particularly, given the University's small size, through those areas in which it was strong; establishing the framework for a sustainable organization; improving facilities for students and staff; and creating a mutually supportive and enriching academic community.

Simultaneously, the way in which the University was managed was overhauled. Senate became the University's principal decision-making body while in January 2005 the eight schools were reduced to four following a decision taken prior to Paul O'Prey's arrival, mainly in response to a less favourable financial settlement from the government. Recognizing the limits of state funding, a Dean of Academic Enterprise was appointed to exploit the economic potential of Roehampton's academic expertise, something many other similar institutions were already doing. A new graduate school was established, with Professor Neil Taylor as Dean of Research. Taylor, well known for his outstanding edition of *Hamlet*, and a long-serving member of staff who had joined Froebel College in 1971, was a former Head of English and Dean of one of the former Faculties. His new post was a formal acknowledgement of the importance of research within Roehampton.

Pro Vice-Chancellor Andy Masheter with Sir Bob Geldof who received an honorary degree for his contribution to social justice in 2007. In his address to students, Geldof said, 'Looking out at you, I'm stunned at how much this University represents this thing that is London, this massive vitality, this huge culture of ideas.'

Above: (From L-R) University Secretary and Registrar Robin Geller, Pro Vice-Chancellor Chris Cobb and Director of Finance Reggie Blennerhassett.

Left: Professor Jane Broadbent, Deputy Vice-Chancellor.

The University's senior management team was restructured and strengthened with external appointments. Dr Peter Briggs OBE, formerly Chief Executive of the British Association for the Advancement of Science, who had become Principal of Southlands in 2002, became one of three new Pro Vice-Chancellors, along with Andy Masheter and Chris Cobb, in September 2005. Andy Masheter joined Roehampton from London South Bank University and his wide-ranging responsibilities, including marketing, international affairs and recruitment, reflected the intention to create a higher profile for the University. Chris Cobb came from the London School of Economics. His expertise in business systems and high-quality IT services were just what Roehampton needed in moving towards a unified organization. After the retirement of Dr Peter Weston in 2005, a new Deputy Vice-Chancellor was appointed

SIR DAVID BELL

David Bell graduated from Cambridge in history and completed a Master's degree at the University of Pennsylvania. Joining the *Financial Times* in 1972, he was appointed Chief Executive in 1993. In 1996 he became a director of Pearson, the major publishing group, and parent of the Financial Times Group, of which he became chairman. He has been involved with a wide range of organizations, including the chairmanship of Sadler's Wells and Crisis, the UK charity of the homeless. As chairman of the Millennium Bridge Trust, he helped to bring about the first new bridge in a century over the Thames in the centre of London. He became Chair of Council at Roehampton in 2008.

January 2006. Professor Jane Broadbent from Royal Holloway College, University of London, was not only an outstanding academic in the field of accountancy but she also had extensive management experience. A new Registrar and Finance Director were also appointed. Robin Geller came as University Secretary from McGill University in Canada, where she was Secretary-General and later took the title Secretary and Registrar; while the new Finance Director, Reggie Blennerhasset, had been in a similar post at the Royal Veterinary College. The creation of this new senior team allowed Roehampton to benefit from the experience gained by each member at other institutions, which opened up many new horizons for the University.

Another significant change in September 2005 came when Baroness Perry stepped down as Chairman of Council. Her replacement was Michael Young, an

Below right: Geoff Thompson MBE (right), five times World Karate Champion, receiving an honorary degree from the University's Chancellor, John Simpson (left), 2008.

JOHN SIMPSON CBE

John Simpson is one of the outstanding international broadcast journalists of his generation. He was educated at St Paul's School and Magdalene College, Cambridge, where he was editor of Granta magazine. Joining the BBC in 1966, he was the Corporation's political editor in 1980–1, diplomatic editor in 1982 and world affairs editor in 1988. Renowned for his overseas reporting, his career has included coverage of many of the major events in recent world history, including accompanying the exiled Ayatollah Khomeini on his return from Paris to Tehran in 1979, the Tiananmen Square massacre in Beijing and the fall of Ceausescu in Romania in 1989, the Gulf War in 1991, the war in Kosovo in 1999, and the invasions of Afghanistan in 2001 and Iraq in 2003. He has received many awards for his work. He became the first Chancellor of Roehampton University in 2005.

Australian-born international businessman and serving member of Council, who proved a great supporter of Roehampton and the ambitious plans of the Vice-Chancellor and his team. In 2008 he was succeeded by Sir David Bell, chairman and former chief executive of the *Financial Times*.

The installation of John Simpson, the distinguished journalist and world affairs editor of the BBC, as the first Chancellor of the new University in November 2005 also did much to raise its profile.

The programme for the continued enhancement of the University's academic standing was wide-ranging and ambitious. It gave a particular boost to specialist areas in which Roehampton was already establishing a respected reputation. In early 2005 the University was awarded a grant of £4.5 million to establish a national Centre of Excellence in teaching human rights (CRUCIBLE). David Woodman was appointed director and CRUCIBLE moved into the Duchesne Building, which was opened by Cherie Booth, QC, the leading human rights lawyer, in November 2006. The building took its name from Rose-Phillippine Duchesne, a member of the Society of the Sacred Heart, who had pioneered free education for native Americans in the early 19th century. An MA in Human Rights Practice was introduced, funded under the European Union's international cooperation programme, Erasmus Mundus, and delivered in partnership with Göteborg University in Sweden and Tromsø University in Norway. A new chair in sociology and social justice was established, and the first holder, appointed in 2007, was Professor Floya Anthias, a respected and widely published sociologist.

Above: The University is set in 54 acres of parkland.

Below: Cherie Booth QC received an honorary degree from Roehampton in 2008 for her work as a leading human rights lawyer, shown here with Robin Geller.

An important part of this was the module entitled Questioning Citizenship, introduced in September 2006. Encompassing topics such as citizenship and film, women as citizens and non-citizens, the status and rights of children, and ethnicity and minority rights, the module was taught to a majority of the University's first-year students.

Under Professor Stephanie Jordan, Director of the Centre for Dance Research, dance maintained its outstanding reputation. Music and dance once again secured the top ranking in the 2008 RAE. Professor Jordan was internationally renowned, in particular for her work on Stravinsky. She was also one of three Roehampton academics who were members of RAE panels, the others being Jane Broadbent and Professor Ann MacLarnon. Professor MacLarnon, who joined Roehampton in 1989, is a renowned anthropologist. Director of the University's world-leading Centre for Research in Evolutionary Anthropology, and currently President of the Primate Society of Great Britain, her research interests encompass both primate biology and palaeoanthropology. Her team has field sites in Nigeria, Puerto Rico and Brazil and has conducted internationally regarded research into human evolution and primatology.

Education too strengthened its reputation. Partnership was often the key to further progress, as in many other areas at Roehampton. A joint doctorate in Education was introduced with Kingston University in 2004. An MA in Special Educational Needs

Below: Professor Ann MacLarnon, the Director of The Centre for Research in Evolutionary Anthropology (CREA) which was set up in 2002. The Centre is considered the top place for biological anthropology research in the UK.

Below right: Teaching at Overton Grammar School.

Left: Primary education.

Below: Film studies.

Bottom: Zachary Leader, Professor of English Literature and respected biographer.

was established in 2005 through the Erasmus Mundus programme in association with Fontys University in the Netherlands and Charles University in Prague. Early Childhood Studies, already a distinctive part of Roehampton's offering, continued to expand in scope, under the direction of two distinguished Professors of Early Childhood Studies, Kevin Brehony, Director of the Centre for Early Childhood Studies, and Tina Bruce, whose national and international contribution to the subject would earn her the award of the CBE in 2009. One innovation was offering professionals involved with young children the chance to take up a placement as part of their course, at children's centres, hospitals, prisons and women's refuges. Roehampton also introduced a Foundation Degree for professionals. This was also achieved through partnership, this time with Carshalton College, where Roehampton validated a two-year foundation course, leading to a third year at Roehampton. In 2008 Roehampton also had one of the highest concentrations of National Teaching Fellows of any university in the country.

One of the striking characteristics of Roehampton is the depth of the distinguished contribution made by academics in many different spheres. Zachary Leader, Professor of English Literature, and a Fellow of the Royal Society of Literature, won international acclaim for his biography of Kingsley Amis, nominated for a Pulitzer Prize in 2008, and was invited to write the authorized biography of Saul Bellow. Jennifer Coates, Professor of English Language and Linguistics, and a Fellow of the English Association, was also internationally renowned in her field, in which she launched a research centre in 2007. In the same year she received from her peers the great honour of a Festschrift for her contribution to linguistics. Nicola Humble, Professor of English Literature, published a well-received book on the history of British cooking, while Graham White, Reader in Drama, was writing widely for theatre, television and radio. Ros Coward, Professor of Journalism, contributed towards an authorized biography of Nelson Mandela. Professor John Tosh became one of the most recognized names in the historical profession. His *The Pursuit of History* went into five editions and was translated into six languages, including Chinese. Also in history, Professor Trevor Dean was winning plaudits for his work on the Italian Renaissance and medieval crime and justice. The range of books published by Roehampton academics was extensive. In 2007 they ranged from the cinema of Lars von Trier and introduction to Francophone literature to a study of 19th-century childhood as seen through children's literature. Among those also singled out for praise were *Time, Religion and History*, the work of Dr William Gallois, Reader in History, and *In The Key of Genius*, written by Adam Ockelford, Professor of Music.

Below right: Dance studies.

Bottom: Professor Cecilia Essau, Director of Centre for Applied Research and Assessment in Child and Adolescent Wellbeing.

This published work was the fruit of the research culture now firmly embedded at Roehampton. The University consciously set out to recruit able young academics at the outset of their careers to enhance the contribution already being made by distinguished long-serving staff. New research centres included those for Scientific and Cultural Research into Sport, Research in Sex, Gender and Sexuality and the Study Of Voluntary and Community Activity. In 2004 the Social Research Centre was set up with Dr Stephen Driver as its first director, conducting policy-based projects for clients in the public and voluntary sectors, as well as academic research and postgraduate study. In 2006 Cecilia Essau, Professor of Developmental Psychopathology, was appointed to lead analytical research in two projects awarded funding of $15 million at the Oregon Research Institute in the USA. Appointed in 2004, Professor Essau had gained an international reputation for her work on anxiety and addiction among children and adolescents. Brought up in a traditional village longhouse in the Borneo jungle, her childhood influenced her views on life: 'To be raised in a longhouse means having to learn to respect the other members of the longhouse (not just my own family members), to learn to share and to keep a harmonious relationship with nature as we believe that every living thing has a soul and a "life"'. In 2007 Barry O'Sullivan, Professor of Applied Linguistics, was invited to design English language tests for use in British Council centres all over the world. Above all, Roehampton's performance in the 2008 RAE showed another significant advance. This was a real watershed in the academic development of the University, marking it out as one of the leading new universities for research. Roehampton had submitted for this Research Assessment more than half of its staff, one of the highest proportions of any modern university. A third of this research was judged either 'world-leading' or 'internationally excellent'. Biological anthropology and dance were rated the best in their subject in the country.

One innovation was the creation of Professorial Fellows in 2008, intended to bring to Roehampton leading figures in various fields. The first of these were Dame Jacqueline Wilson and Professor Allan Hobson. As one of the world's most successful children's writers, Jacqueline Wilson teaches regularly on the Children's Literature and Creative Writing programmes offered by the University. Professor Hobson, Professor Emeritus of the Harvard Medical School, is best known for his pioneering work on the neurobiology of rapid eye movement (REM) sleep and has made a major

LUCY WHELAN, PRESIDENT OF THE STUDENTS' UNION, 2005

Lucy Whelan came to Roehampton at the age of 18 in 2000 to study dance, attracted by the campus and the location so close to London. Quickly becoming involved with the Students' Union, she was later elected Vice-President and took over as President during her final sabbatical year. This was during Roehampton's transition to full university status so, as well as maintaining day-to-day links with fellow students, she was involved with many of the key decisions being taken at the time. She always felt that the opinions of the students were appreciated and in particular valued the interest taken by the newly appointed Pro Vice-Chancellors in student affairs. University status enhanced the role of the Union as an organization which brought together students as a whole from all over the University. The move of Whitelands to Parkstead and the concentration of student resources at the heart of the campus also helped to bring students closer together. Yet she always valued the individuality of the colleges, describing them as a unique selling point for the University, emphasizing Roehampton's diversity while contributing towards its harmony. Lucy, who left to become a freelance television researcher, believes the university in general gave her 'a lesson in life that was invaluable'; while Roehampton in particular 'made me who I am today, it shaped me, it made me confident and ambitious and proud of where I studied'.

Paul O'Prey, the Vice-Chancellor, and Lucy Whelan.

Warming up in front of Parkstead House.

contribution towards increasing knowledge of how the brain regulates sleep, waking and consciousness. Over three years he will deliver a number of seminars and lectures in a series named after the philosopher William James.

As well as the quality of the teaching and research at Roehampton, the recruitment of students also depended upon the quality of the facilities. The University needed what the Vice-Chancellor called 'a fully integrated student strategy'. One change quickly initiated by Paul O'Prey was the rationalization of an unwieldy curriculum, which was reduced from some 1500 options in 2004 to just over 400 three years later. In response to student satisfaction surveys, academic support for students was increased with an enhanced personal tutor scheme, the library was refurbished, and on-line learning facilities were improved, with all bedrooms in the colleges equipped with internet access. In 2008 the University was one of the first in the country to become 100 per cent 'wireless'. The results of all this were seen in the review carried out by the Quality Assurance Agency for Higher Education in 2008, which recognized the commitment of staff to teaching and learning as well as their wider efforts to support students.

Initiatives were launched to improve the quality of student life. One focus was the physical and spiritual wellbeing of students. In 2007 Ian Pickup became the first Director of Sport and Wellbeing, implementing a strategy which covered not just sporting activities and facilities but also aspects such as health, nutrition and welfare. Following the success of offering the Questioning Citizenship module to all new students, a Wellbeing and Lifestyle module was introduced on the same basis. Sport Roehampton was formed to promote team and individual sporting activities and exercise. University teams received professional coaching and students were given the chance to take part in more sports, such as volleyball, women's gymnastics and tae kwon do. A new gym was opened, multi-purpose outdoor sports facilities

were developed, more sports pitches were leased and, in partnership with the local authority, the University contributed towards the refurbishment of the local sports centre in Wandsworth. A Health and Wellbeing Adviser was appointed, the posts of Student Welfare Officers became full-time and the range of University counselling services was expanded. The College chaplains, now including Hindu, Muslim and Jewish as well as Christian chaplains, were an important part of this support. The post of chaplaincy coordinator was created and an inter-faith festival was initiated in 2006. A Muslim Liaison Officer was appointed in 2007 to advise on support for the growing number of Muslim students, in line with the University's policy of diversity.

Intertwined with all this was the action taken by the University to adopt a sustainable and environmentally positive approach to the way Roehampton was run. Situated on a campus whose natural environment was second to none compared with similar institutions in the London area, Roehampton developed a series of policies to promote greater awareness of biodiversity. The interrelationship between social responsibility and sustainable development was embodied in a special committee set up to consider both issues, chaired by the Vice-Chancellor. An environmental forum was established, which helped to secure Fairtrade status for the University, a campaign backed by the Student Union, which also organized its own Go Green initiative. Students even organized a petition asking the Vice-Chancellor to appoint

Roehampton University cheerleaders, the Roehampton Rascals, have won a national reputation in this new competitive sport.

The Learning Resources Centre at the centre of the campus offers books and journals, electronic editions, databases, DVD, internet, PC suites, Wired social learning space, an internet café and much, much more.

an Environmental Officer; his response was to appoint not one but two. All this helped to enhance the quality of life for all those involved within the University.

Together with a host of other improvements, all this helped to increase the number of applications to the University and reduce the student drop-out rate. In 2007 for the first time Roehampton was no longer dependent on clearing to fill places. With a higher profile and a growing reputation, the University was attracting a higher proportion of more able students. It also helped that nearly 90 per cent of Roehampton graduates found employment within six months of leaving university. The University was also taking more students from across the UK rather than being reliant on a local catchment area. In 2007 four out of five new students reported a positive first impression of Roehampton while a survey of all students revealed more than 80 per cent were satisfied with the quality of their course and their overall experience. There was also a steady improvement in the percentage of those content with campus life.

Roehampton also wanted to share its advantages with the local community, which at the same time also helped to make the University better known. The Sport and Wellbeing Strategy was exported beyond the boundaries of the University through the creation of a Community Sports Development Officer. As well as being the joint sponsor of the Enterprising Roehampton Awards, the University was involved in a variety of education, health and sporting projects with neighbouring boroughs. One project, partly funded by the National Froebel Foundation, based on sport and the community, aimed to help disadvantaged children widen their horizons. It illustrated perfectly the way in which Roehampton sought to draw together the University's expertise for the benefit of students and others.

The University was also engaged in a variety of partnerships overseas. While bringing advantages to Roehampton's partners, these relationships also helped to raise more money for the University. As well as participating in the Erasmus Mundus scheme, they have included health and education projects in India, including the development of the first mental health institute in the state of Gujarat; collaboration over teacher training with the Universiti Pendidikan Sultan Idris in Malaysia; and an agreement with the College of Technology at Vietnam National University in Hanoi. The University was also reaping the benefits of its International Centre, set up in

Left: Dame Jaqueline Wilson, Professorial Fellow.
Below: Graduation at Guildford Cathedral.

2002, which regularly sent representatives to overseas fairs and on visits to schools and colleges in other countries. Roehampton continued to be successful in recruiting students from countries like India and China, the USA and Mexico, which also brought in additional revenue. For the Vice-Chancellor, creating this international focus for the University was a key priority and in just one academic year Paul O'Prey's overseas visits encompassed Israel and the Palestinian Territories, Bulgaria, Singapore – where he accompanied the UK Minister for Higher Education – and India.

Huge progress was accomplished in securing the important objective of a unified campus while at the same time establishing a new relationship with the colleges. The Vice-Chancellor wrote in January 2006 how 'Roehampton's four colleges have helped to define not only its history, but also its character and core values, which in turn will continue to inform the University's future'. The development of education and human rights, for instance, and the extension of the University's links with developing countries were a testament to this. By then, two landmarks had been achieved: firstly, Whitelands had at last moved to Parkstead House; and secondly, and perhaps more importantly, a ground-breaking agreement had been made between the University and the Froebel Educational Institute as the providing body of Froebel College. The Institute recognized that it was only through the University that the legacy of Friedrich Froebel could be effectively sustained on the Institute's behalf. A 999-year lease of the College buildings was agreed between the Institute and the University, while maintaining the Froebel name. This highlighted the fact that the agreement was as much to the advantage of the College as to the University. It effectively bound them both together by making the University the long-term defender of the distinctive nature of the College. For the University, this was the first step towards assuming overall responsibility for the entire campus. In 2008 the agreement formed the template for a similar lease between the University and the Society of the Sacred Heart in relation to Digby Stuart College for a term of 125 years. As with Froebel, the University agreed to preserve the name and the ethos of the College. This included the launch of a million-pound scholarship fund, the inauguration of an annual Digby Stuart lecture and the creation of a Research Centre for Catholic Studies, with Tina Beattie as the first

professor. Negotiations on the same lines are continuing with the providing bodies of Southlands and Whitelands.

Well before the timespan of the Vice-Chancellor's first strategic plan had expired, many of its objectives had either been achieved or were close to being achieved. There were neverthess several areas where there was scope for considerable future improvement. Major investment was needed in the campus, particularly the provision of a new library and learning resources. This was one of several areas in which Roehampton, in spite of recent improvements, still lagged behind other institutions in meeting the needs and expectations of students. As a result, in 2009, the University welcomed the Vice-Chancellor's next strategy paper. Looking forward to the University's 21st birthday, 'Roehampton 2025' gave the University two decades to come of age. It foresaw a university which had maintained a distinctive identity and built on past achievements to acquire an international reputation for learning and teaching in key areas, to rank among the top third of universities in the UK in terms of research and to become one of the top ten universities in the UK for student satisfaction. It was an ambitious prescription but, given the rapid progress achieved by Roehampton since it became an independent university, it was also one whose attainment seemed possible.

As the first decade of the 21st century came to a close, Roehampton University was already well established among the ranks of the UK's modern universities. Although it was only half a dozen years old, it had made this transition partly thanks to the long history of its constituent colleges. They lent the University much of its character. This came not just from their physical presence, ranging from the attractive modern buildings of Southlands on the Roehampton Lane campus to the stately splendour of Whitelands at Parkstead. It was felt also in the University's leading reputation in the field of education, where it drew on traditions stretching back to the first half of the 19th century. It was also apparent in the humane ethos

prevailing at Roehampton, derived in part from the feminine liberalism which had influenced the colleges, still sustained today when three-quarters of all students are women. And it can be seen in the standing the University has earned in areas like social justice, human rights and religion, which again owes so much to the traditions of the four colleges.

The critical act of faith made by the colleges in coming together in adverse circumstances to create the Roehampton Institute of Higher Education in 1975 showed the power of cooperation, a lesson which was not forgotten in subsequent years. The work of the Institute under successive Rectors, all of whom shared a vision of Roehampton as an independent university, paved the way for the new University's second Vice-Chancellor and his team to begin shaping Roehampton into a truly holistic organization. In remarkably quick time Roehampton has not only sustained its reputation for teaching but combined with it a growing reputation for research, producing in

Above: The entrance to Whitelands.
Right: The Whitelands Clock.

several areas some outstanding work. The University has also remained true to its heritage in the composition of its student body. Just as with the first colleges, many of Roehampton's students are young women from disadvantaged backgrounds given an opportunity for an education never contemplated by their parents. Yet Roehampton today is more than the sum of its parts, offering a richer and more varied learning environment than would ever have been possible for any of the colleges to provide. All this has been accomplished at the end of just the first stage in Roehampton's growth as a university. Like a fine wine, the University has yet to reach maturity, but the ambitious future path it has set itself for the years ahead is clearly marked out. It should be a great vintage.

Overleaf: The Duchesne Building, a state-of-the-art teaching facility housing the Crucible, a national centre of excellence for human rights education.

Below: Graduation day.

INDEX

BIBLIOGRAPHY

Aldrich, Richard, *The Institute of Education 1902–2002, A centenary history*, London, 2002

Burgess, Keith, *History of Roehampton University*, typescript, n.d. (Southlands College Archive)

Cole, Malcolm, *Whitelands College – The History*, Whitelands College Monographs, No 2, 1982

Edwards, Elizabeth, *Women in Teacher Training Colleges 1900–1960, A Culture of Feminity*, London, 2001

Foster, Eileen, *Digby-Stuart College, Roehampton, 1946–1975*, typescript, 2001 (Digby College Archive)

Foster, Eileen, *St Charles' College, Kensington, 1905–1946*, typescript, 1999 (Digby College Archive)

Foster, Eileen, *Training College of the Sacred Heart for Catholic Schoolmistresses, West Hill, Wandsworth, 1874–1904*, typescript, 1995 (Digby College Archive)

Ludlow, May, *Southlands: A Moving Story*, typescript, 2003 (Soutlands College Archive)

Millbank, Douglas, *Years of Change: A History of Southlands College 1970–1985*, 1985

O'Leary, April, *Living Tradition, The Chronicle of a School, Roehampton-Woldingham 1842–1992*, Greenford, 1992

Seed, John, *Training Female School Teachers in Victorian London: A Study of Three Colleges*, typescript, 1995–6 (This can also be found at www.billygriff.sathosting.net/seed)

The Froebel Educational Institute – A Centenary Review, 1892–1992

Weston, Peter, *From Roehampton Great House to Grove House to Froebel College – An Illustrated History*, London, 1998

Weston, Peter, *The Froebel Educational Institute, the Origins and History of the College*, 2002

Williams, Eva, *The History of Southlands College 1872–1972*, London, 1972

PICTURE ACKNOWLEDGEMENTS

Roehampton University and TMI Publishers would like to thank all the photographers whose work has been reproduced in this book. Most of the images came from the college archives and from the University's collection of modern photographs. In addition we are grateful to the following for allowing us to reproduce the following images: p44 (top left) Pete Shacky, Berlin; p51 (top) The Granger Collection/ TopFoto, (bottom) ©Bettmann/Corbis; p56 The Northern Echo (Newsquest Northeast) Ltd; p96 Topfoto.

From	To	Daily Routine	Days	From	To	Class I	From
VI.	VII.	Rise, wash, dress and sweep Rooms		IX.50	10.30	Grammar Lesson.	IX.
				X.30	XI.40	Reading.	X.
VII.	VII.50	Scripture Lesson.	Monday.	XI.40	I.	Arithmetic. Mr Tate.	XI.
				II.	II.50	Needle-work.	
VII.50	VIII.30	Morning Prayers.		II.30	III.30	Singing. Mr May.	II.
VIII.30	IX.	Breakfast.		III.30	V.	Needle-work.	III.
IX.	IX.50	Recreation and Household work.		IX.50	X.30	Geography Lesson.	IX.
				X.30	XI.20	Paraphrase.	X.
IX.50	I.	Lessons and Recreation.	Tuesday.	XI.20	XII.	Reading.	XI.
				I.30	III.	Needle-work.	I.
I.	I.30	Dinner		III.	III.50	History Lesson.	III.
I.30	I.30½.II.	Recreation		III.50	IV.30	Copy Books.	III.
I.30 or II	III.30	Needle work and Singing Lesson		IX.50	XI.15	Lesson with Revd H. Baber	IX.
			Wednesday.	XI.15	XII.	Grammar Lesson.	XI.
III.30	V.	Studies.		II.	III.30	Lesson with Mr Hullah	II.
V.	V.30	Tea.		III.30	V.	Needle-work.	III.
V.30	VI.	Recreation		IX.50	X.30	Geography Lesson.	IX.
				X.30	X.50	Poetry.	X.
VI.	VII.	Drilling Master and Practise Singing		X.50	I.	Arithmetic. Mr Tate.	X.
			Thursday.	II.	II.30	Needle-work.	II.
				II.30	III.30	Singing. Mr May.	II.
				III.30	IV.30	Model Lesson	II.
VII.	VII.30	Evening Prayers		IV.30	V.	Write an Exercise	IV.30
VII.30	VIII.	Prepare Lessons.		IX.50	X.30	Grammar Lesson.	IX.
				X.30	XI.10	History.	X.
VIII	VIII.15	Supper.	Friday.	XI.10	XII.	Reading.	XI.
VIII.15	IX.	Finish Lessons.		II.	III.	Needle-work.	II.
at	IX.	Go to Bed.		III.	IV.	Revd H. Baber's Exercise	III.
				IV.	IV.30	Copy Books.	IV.